PREPARE FOR
Purpose
YOUR INVITATION TO THE NEXT LEVEL

Compiled by Sharvette Mitchell

CHANDRA BROADNAX-PAYNE, DANA WILSON,
DESIREÉ HARRIS-BONNER, EZREAONNE JACKSON,
JOICE SAWYER, LYNN LEWIS, ROZ BROWN,
DR. TABATHA M. W. SPURLOCK, AND DR. TSCHANNA TAYLOR

Prepare for Purpose: Your Invitation to the Next Level

Copyright © 2023 Sharvette Mitchell

All rights reserved. No part of this book may be reproduced, stored, or transmitted by any means—whether auditory, graphic, mechanical, or electronic—without written permission of both publisher and author, except in the case of brief excerpts used in critical articles and reviews. Unauthorized reproduction of any part of this work is illegal and is punishable by law.

Scriptures marked KJV are taken from the KING JAMES VERSION (KJV): KING JAMES VERSION, public domain.

Scripture taken from the New King James Version®. Copyright © 1982 by Thomas Nelson. Used by permission. All rights reserved.

Scripture quotations taken from the Amplified® Bible (AMP), Copyright © 2015 by The Lockman Foundation. Used by permission. www.lockman.org

Scripture quotations marked (NLT) are taken from the Holy Bible, New Living Translation, copyright ©1996, 2004, 2015 by Tyndale House Foundation. Used by permission of Tyndale House Publishers, Carol Stream, Illinois 60188. All rights reserved.

Scripture quotations marked (TLB) are taken from The Living Bible, copyright © 1971 by Tyndale House Foundation. Used by permission of Tyndale House Publishers, Carol Stream, Illinois 60188. All rights reserved.

Lyrics for "No Greater Love" by David L. Allen used with permission per Co-Author Roz Brown.

Lyrics for "For a Little Bit of Love" by Chief Apostle Olive C. Brown used with permission per Co-Author Roz Brown.

Published by:
Mitchell Productions, LLC
www.Mitchell-Productions.com

Cover photography
Kimie James

Anthology Editor
Chandra Sparks Splond, M.S.E.
www.chandrasparkssplond.com

Book Creation and Design
DHBonner Virtual Solutions, LLC
www.dhbonner.net

ISBN for print version: 978-1-7333754-9-8
ISBN for hardcover version: 979-8-9876197-0-4
ISBN for eBook version: 979-8-9876197-1-1

Printed in the United States of America

To my faith leaders, Chief Apostle Olive C. Brown, Bishop Joel V. Brown and my church family at New Jerusalem International Chrisitian Ministries... your support and encouragement have been a constant source of inspiration and strength to me throughout my journey to purpose.

Table of Contents

Introduction vii

Recalculating: When Vision Meets Purpose 1
DR. TSCHANNA TAYLOR

Choosing to thrive in the Aftermath 11
LYNN LEWIS

Every Strand Counts 23
DANA WILSON

No More Running 33
DR. TABATHA M. W. SPURLOCK

Directing Your Path to Purpose 43
CHANDRA BROADNAX-PAYNE

Processed for a Purpose 53
DESIREÉ HARRIS-BONNER

Positioned for Purpose 63
JOICE M. SAWYER

Purpose is a Journey to be Lived 75
EZREAONNE JACKSON

Love on Purpose 87
ROZ BROWN

Your Exit Strategy 107
SHARVETTE MITCHELL

Introduction

In 2002, *The Purpose Driven Life* by Pastor Rick Warren hit the bookstore shelves. This book seemed to come on the scene with a fury and had everyone talking about purpose. People began asking about and trying to discover the purpose for their life. Although it is a bible study book, I can remember hearing about this book everywhere. According to Wikipedia, the book topped the Wall Street Journal best seller charts as well as Publishers Weekly charts. *The Purpose Driven Life* was on the New York Times Bestseller List for over 90 weeks. According to both the author and publisher Simon & Schuster, 50 million copies had been sold in more than 85 languages by 2020.

Clearly this book struck a nerve and started a lot of conversations and thoughts about purpose. What is my purpose? How do I identify my purpose? How do I live in my purpose? The list of questions about the topic of purpose goes on. Here's what I don't hear a lot about… how to prepare for purpose.

To illustrate why we should also focus on preparation, let me draw your attention to the butterfly. Although not seen often, the butterfly can capture and hold your attention as you get mesmerized by its beauty. Even if it is a few fleeting moments, you remember your encounter with a beautiful butterfly. What did it take for that butterfly to become so amazing and captivating? Perhaps a better question is how did the caterpillar prepare to become a butterfly?

Metamorphosis is the process of transformation from a caterpillar to its end purpose of a butterfly. Here are the stages of metamorphosis with the associated timeframes:

Egg: The female butterfly lays eggs on a suitable plant. The time from egg laying to hatching can range from **a few days to several weeks.**

Caterpillar: The egg hatches into a caterpillar, which feeds on plant leaves and grows rapidly. The caterpillar stage can last from **a few weeks to several months.**

Pupa: The caterpillar molts several times and eventually forms a pupa or chrysalis. The pupal stage typically lasts from **several days to several weeks**, depending on the species and environmental conditions.

Butterfly: The pupa transforms into a butterfly through metamorphosis, with its body and wings changing and maturing. The butterfly emerges from the pupa, expands its wings and flies away.

The lifespan of most butterflies is **only 2 to 3 weeks**, but this can vary greatly among species.

If you add up the time the butterfly spent in preparing for its purpose (i.e., several months) compared to the beautiful emergence of the end state (i.e., 2 to 3 weeks life span), it is a clear indicator that our life's purpose is really about the journey and not just the destination.

In "Prepare for Purpose," we guide readers on a journey of self-discovery and reflection, helping them to identify how their life experiences and faith strengthen their purpose. Whether you are just beginning to explore the concept of purpose or you are well on your way to fulfilling your own, this book is an invaluable resource for recognizing your unique path and creating a fulfilling life.

Sharvette Mitchell
Visionary Author

PREPARE FOR *Purpose*
YOUR INVITATION TO THE NEXT LEVEL

Recalculating: When Vision Meets Purpose

DR. TSCHANNA TAYLOR

It's a busy Saturday morning, and I am preparing for my inaugural women's event. I'm so exhausted from the night before decorating, moving tables, and making sure everything is just right. I'm rushing to get dressed because it's almost time for me to be at the hotel to serve my guests. My hair won't stay pinned, and I have already made a run in my stockings in a rush to get ready. My son is starting to anger me because he hasn't even gotten dressed yet, and we are running out of time. I'm all over the place, and my phone is ringing off the hook from my assistant calling to see what's my location. I'm finally all set and ready to go to the hotel.

As I walk out of the house, I heard the news station mention the interstate I usually travel had a five-car pileup on Interstate 85. I'm thinking, *Lord, I don't need this now.* I put the address in my GPS to find a better way to get there without hitting the traffic. I enter the hotel's location, and Grace (the name I have given my GPS) tells me, "We're all set; let's get ready to go." She then tells me to proceed 675 feet toward the right of my driveway to turn right onto the main street. I'm in my Jeep with the air blasting because it's hot outside, and I do not need any more hair issues or my makeup to mess up.

Then Grace tells me, "In 2.4 miles, go east on North Duke Street." But I wasn't paying attention for jamming to my music loud, feeling good about today's event that's about to take place, and I miss my turn. Grace blurts out, "Recalculating." I'm fussing now because I have added more time to my commute, which will make me late to get to my event. Thank God I decorated the night before. Luckily, I had two hours before the event started and planned for just-in-case moments such as this slight detour. I believe in being on time, but I was failing this day. I eventually made it to the hotel to answer questions from my assistant and do last-minute touchups before the event got started. Thank God everything turned out lovely, and the audience created new memories of networking and fellowshipping with one another.

Think about your routes to work, church, or even the grocery store. You could probably take multiple ways but stick to that one route. It's quick, efficient, and becomes routine for you. We get to the point of not even thinking of the route; we get there and realize we weren't actively aware of the entire drive. We know the path works well, and we stick to it.

What makes this route unique anyway? Is it the number of lanes, stoplights, and the timing of the stoplights? On any given day, the right way could change; over time, it could evolve. The identity of the route hasn't changed—it can get you to your favorite grocery store—but for each season of life, the correct way may be different.

We agree that everything was created with intent and purpose, regardless of our journey—you were and I was. We were made for much more than a stressful job and miserable relationships. Just like the trusted route you use to get to where you are going, there are components of who you are that have been there from the beginning and others that developed over time.

It's like you wanting to book a flight to your favorite tropical island. You must select when booking your departure city and your destination city. Once you know where you want to go, the travel site provides a list of airlines that will take you there, at what time, and how much the trip will cost. You start "here," but the goal is to end up "there." There, which is the destination city, is a place of destiny. We were all meant to become who God created us to be on earth. The journey you and I are on now is a place that begins with here—the starting point, the process, the cost—and there, or the ending point. We must be clear about our location to get from here to there.

We use a GPS to help guide us to where we want to go, providing us with the safest way to get there. Life is like the GPS. We have people in our lives—from coaches, family members, ministry leaders, and friends—guiding us in the directions we should take. I don't know about you, but I have ventured off and gotten sidetracked many times. God always knows how to "recalculate" us to get us back on track. Can you imagine what your life would be like just relying only on a physical map? I know for me, sometimes maps were hard to read or understand, so whenever I traveled, I would stop at the convenience store to get directions on how to get to where I was going before GPS was created. Thank God for technology.

Sometimes the GPS can give us wrong directions that can cause us to get lost or possibly put us in some dangerous situations. It is similar with us making bad decisions or taking the wrong advice from others. The good news is that when you make the wrong turn or wrong decision, you can decide to do things differently. No matter how often you make a mistake, your GPS (purpose) will recalculate for you.

The path you take on this journey called life—whether it's friendship, marriage, or business—will not come without mistakes or "detours." We want to think that the journey will be easy, but it is not. Only when we seek to learn to do better, apply what we know, and move forward, do we find success in whatever it is we are trying to achieve. We all must recalculate from time to time.

Let me share my experience with recalculating and how vision met with my purpose. I have been in business since I was eighteen years old. My first business was desktop publishing. I learned a lot from the mistakes of giving my products and services away for free, not following up with customers or understanding the actual work involved with being an entrepreneur. Life happened, and even if I wanted to walk away from entrepreneurship, I couldn't.

Life's lessons have taught me to be clear on where I am currently, know where I want to go or have a good idea, and be willing to go through a process and pay the price. Once you leave your comfort zone, you will enjoy the rewards of your journey. Trust me, there were a lot of uncomfortable moments, but it made me who I am today personally and professionally.

These are new and changing times. Sometimes they feel uncertain with everything happening in the world today. I understand, and it can feel overwhelming with so much pain, anger, and frustration. I know a lot of uncertainty around us might make you question if this is the right time to step out of your comfort zone.

With the price increase in everything, people losing their jobs, and the threat of a recession closing in on us, I know that you would instead stick to what you know and understand now. I cannot fault you for that, and I understand what that is like.

I have a full-time corporate job that I love, a business that I am dedicated to, and a son whom I would sacrifice anything for. That is why the past few weeks had me in my thinking place, and I have been pondering the best way to ride out this period and come out on the other side bigger and better.

As I worked on adjusting here and there, I realized that I wouldn't have the luxury of keeping my job, thriving at my business, and raising the most fantastic son if I had not decided some years ago to live my life with a vision—not just my dream, but a vision that answered God's calling for my life.

Today, all I stand on is my faith in God and the vision He has given me. In 2020, my son's tragic fall in our home resulted in a severe concussion and seizures in the middle of a pandemic.

Now imagine going through this experience with the doctors taking more precedence with the newly diagnosed COVID-19 patients than helping save my son's life. We waited in the intensive care unit for days, praying and calling on Jesus to heal him. He didn't even remember I was Momma. I was devastated. Plus, I was married to a veteran with post-traumatic stress disorder who blamed himself for the accident. It was no one's fault, and it was just that, an accident. As the encourager and caregiver I had always been, I had to be there for my husband and son. I was stretched in many directions, letting myself go in the process. Sitting in the waiting room allowed me time to pray, but I also reflected on how I even got here in the first place.

Remember I shared with you earlier how I had been in business since I was eighteen years old, which was well over twenty-eight years ago? (Side note: And I am not that old. Smile.) I got married for the third time in 2009 while working full-time, and I relaunched my business. I was the women's ministry coordinator, director for Christian education, and worship leader, as well as a wife, mom, sister, and friend. I was always on the go, wearing myself thin. I didn't know what it meant to be well-balanced because I was people pleasing terribly.

Eventually, it took me having multiple health issues to realize I needed to tame the superwoman complex. This syndrome was the driving force for me to do more despite fatigue and countless activities. Unfortunately, this superwoman complex demanded more of me and robbed me of my inner peace, rest, and renewal. How could I be all that God called me to be when the superwoman complex served as a rigid taskmaster? I was always at some conference, networking event, or having my classes to teach individuals how to write and publish their books to create additional streams of income.

I didn't realize how it cost me my marriage, finding out my son was bullied by his teachers and peers, and replenishing myself spiritually, physically, mentally, and emotionally.

After reflecting on how I arrived at this place, my son was discharged from the hospital. Things started to get worse for me after this. Stress can cause so much damage in many areas of our lives.

I was headed to the pharmacy to pick up my son's prescription when I noticed that I kept seeing black spots in my left eye. I didn't think anything of it and kept on about my day. Finally, the black spots got larger and lasted for about two weeks. Now I was nervous and didn't know what to do. I called my brother to share the news with him because my husband has PTSD, and I didn't want to share this with him for him to blame himself. We agreed it would be best to make an eye appointment to check things out.

I made the appointment only to learn that the retina in my left eye had detached. There was a small tear that needed repair. With any surgery, there are risks, including swelling, loss of vision, cataracts, scarring, and more. The surgery was scheduled the day after my son's birthday. The surgery went well. I had strict instructions that required me to sleep straight up in a recliner for two weeks. Talk about being miserable and disgruntled from being unable to get in bed. Three months passed, and I learned at my follow-up appointment that my retina had detached again. I had developed scarring and a cataract that needed to be removed.

I fought hard to keep depression at bay. The Lord knew just what I needed. I couldn't work my corporate job or watch TV because of the surgery, but I could read, write, and participate in a small support group by phone. I met a seventy-three-year-old who experienced the same surgery with her right eye. She encouraged me and motivated me to continue to operate in the calling placed on my life. She reminded me that everything that I had been through, purpose was involved, and it was my responsibility to answer the purpose calling me.

Slowly, I pushed through the pain and hurt I was experiencing with losing sight in my eye, teaching myself how to do the tasks I performed before losing sight. It wasn't easy. I would walk into the poles in the grocery store, walls at home, or sometimes stubbing my toe on the bedpost in the middle of the night for bathroom runs.

I'll never forget doing a Facebook live on my page, sharing my son's experience and my own about losing sight. I received an email from a nonprofit organization asking me to contact the director. I called to inquire how I could be of assistance, only to learn that the nonprofit organization had been following me on social media for some time and wanted to invite me to speak at my first TEDx in Indianapolis, Indiana. I was in awe. In tears, I accepted the opportunity. I knew nothing about how to talk on a TEDx. Thankfully, I completed training as an international speaker in Louisville, Kentucky, seven months before the pandemic. God always knows when you need to be recalculated, right?

I had sixty days to prepare, so I hired a speaking coach. The training was rigorous but necessary. The day that I had to present my speech to my coach was when I heard the Lord tell me that everything I had been through would not be wasted. He told me to name my talk "Although I Lost Sight in One Eye, I Didn't Lose the Vision." The title alone could preach. I met my TEDx peers, and one of the speakers reassured me that God had positioned me for this journey for such a time as this. To my amazement, every speaker there had a story so moving that there were no dry eyes in the audience. I was so encouraged by the responses after giving my speech that I received an opportunity to be featured in a documentary. I am preparing to write a solo book project on losing sight in one eye but still holding on to the vision. I'm still scratching my head and can only say, "God did this."

This entire experience helped me have a clearer vision, one to help me see that my purpose was being fulfilled and why my purpose had to meet with my vision. Being clear about the vision is the only way to reach your purpose. What comes in all shapes and sizes, can be delivered to you anywhere you are, and can affect you when you're asleep or awake?

Distractions can. Distractions often derail our vision and destiny. Just like you take a wrong turn while using the GPS to get to where you're going, distractions can avert your attention from your vision, delay your purpose, destroy your destiny's purpose, and derail your purpose's progress.

Your life's purpose is the catalyst for your vision and dreams. You began your life's journey in God's perfect timing, packed with the unique talents, abilities, gifts, and skills that allow you to make a difference in this world. Whether you know it or not, you've been living out your purpose in many ways. You can't help being you—it's how you were created. Your purpose is like the GPS I described earlier. It keeps you from hitting those detours (distractions like beliefs, status quo, traditions, fear, disobedience, blame, and procrastination). Your purpose guides you toward the places you are created to go. Without this guide, you may waste valuable time, energy, and resources on reaching an area that may not be right for you. Knowing your purpose gives you the direction to create the path He has set with the right vision. When living in alignment with your purpose, your definition of success has a new meaning.

Embracing your purpose gives you the courage to step out of your comfort zone. When we face the detours on our journey, all sorts of fears of the unknown, rejection, and success pop up. Sure, there will be speed bumps and sharp curves, but God won't allow them to derail your progress; hence you are being recalculated.

Begin to appreciate and understand who you are and what matters to you. Only by getting to know who you are can you focus on where you want to go and what you want to do. Reflect on what you have done in your past and ask yourself if you're always taking the same route or if it is time to take a new one. Activate the voice within rather than listening to the noise around you. Seek those who will support you while you are recalculating.

Vision meets purpose when you embrace every circumstance, good or bad, in your life. Take the risks to pursue your dreams, and don't allow fear to hold you back. Reflect on your past, examine your present, and cast a vision for your future without limitations.

Like the GPS, type in where you're going. Nothing happens until you do something (set goals for yourself). Find the best route to get you where you're going—hire a coach, take a course. Receive the updates on how far you must go—read as much as possible, implement what you're learning. Recalculate often. Life will throw you curves, but you have the flexibility to keep moving forward—don't stay stuck. Be okay if you make a wrong turn—there's always a blessing in the lesson. You won't get it right all the time, but don't beat yourself up about it either.

Do you need to recalculate in your life? This is how you recalculate. Where are you now? Where do you want to go? How will you get there? What is the process you must face? What is the cost? Examining these questions can help you determine your purpose.

Dr. Tschanna Taylor

Whereas others find their greatest fulfillment and motivation in moving forward, she found hers in looking back. Affectionately known as Dr. Tee, Dr. Tschanna Taylor realized to effectively build, she had to heal hurts and wounds that stemmed from as far back as childhood. As an entrepreneur, for over twenty-eight years, she's committed to helping others dig through roots in their life and confidently share their message to grow and bear fruits monetizing from their pain.

Tschanna is a publisher, TEDx speaker, marketplace chaplain, and authorpreneur. Tschanna holds several degrees and certifications from Villanova University, Keller Graduate School of Management, Liberty University, and other institutions, focusing on entrepreneurship. Set apart by her transparent delivery and transformative storytelling abilities, anyone can clearly see that she is resilient about helping others operate authentically and unapologetically in their purpose.

Visit her website at www.tschannataylor.com
or contact her at info@tschannataylor.com

Choosing to thrive in the Aftermath

LYNN LEWIS

"Lord, prepare me for whatever this day has in store for me" was the breath prayer I uttered as I pulled out of my driveway on Monday morning, July 29, 2019. I had no inkling it would play out to be the prelude to the worst week of my life, culminating on the worst day of my life.

Turn your pain to purpose is a statement I have heard used over the years as it relates to learning to navigate life after it has been disrupted by a riveting experience. While I had been faced with and triumphed through a great many challenges during my lifetime, nothing prepared me for the one that was waiting in the balance for me. I had never given thought to the possibility of ever having the opportunity to really know the magnitude of what turning your pain to purpose could be like until it happened.

The breath prayer that morning related to me traveling approximately sixty-five miles from my home in Richmond, Virginia, to a hospital in

Newport News, Virginia, to be with my brother, Troy. He was there to receive his first of several chemotherapy infusions. We settled into the amply furnished, well-lit, cool room. The staff was attentive and cordial to their patients and guests.

My brother and I were chatting as we normally do when we are together while waiting for his labs to be released signaling to his nurse the okay to start his infusion. No sooner than he and I had finished talking about my son, Daniel, and how much he seemed to like working for the City of Richmond Fire Department where he had been employed for eleven months, my phone rang. It was Daniel's dad and my husband, Keith. I wondered aloud why he would be calling because he knew I was with Troy in the infusion lab. He proceeded to tell me, per the phone call he received from his crew at the fire station, Daniel did not report for his shift that morning nor was he responding to phone calls or text messages. The crew was concerned because that was not typical behavior for Daniel.

I recalled that Daniel told me on the prior Thursday that he was getting someone to take his Monday shift because he had a mandatory appointment that evening (he worked twenty-four-hour shifts). He told his dad via text on the day before we received the call that he had worked it out. If that had been the case, his crew would have been aware of the change. Daniel was a professional firefighter. It is not a job where you do not show up because you do not "feel like" working on a particular day. Outside of it being an emergency, it just does not happen.

We, along with his crew, attempted many times throughout the day to reach him by phone to no avail. He worked for the City of Richmond but lived in the Newport News area. The hospital was only about ten minutes away from Daniel's apartment, so I drove there to hopefully see him and find out why he had not reported to work.

When I arrived at his apartment, his vehicle was parked directly in front of his building. I remember when I saw the vehicle, my heart began to beat so fast it felt like it would literally beat right through the wall of my chest. I did not have a key, so I knocked and knocked and called his name asking him to let me in, to no avail. Because this behavior was out of character for Daniel, we contacted the police department to do a welfare check. He was nowhere to be found inside.

Where could my child be? Had he gone out for a walk the night before and someone had robbed and beat him up and left him for dead? Was he in some type of trouble that no one close to him knew about? Those and a million other questions ran through my mind for the next six days.

We had no idea where he was until six days later—Sunday night, August 4. Authorities from City of Richmond fire and police departments visited our home to tell us his body had been found in Mecklenburg County, Charlotte, North Carolina.

What?

"Are you sure?" is the question I asked the City of Richmond detective at least ten times. I had to know for sure before I made any phone calls to family members and friends who had been anxiously awaiting to hear from Daniel along with us.

The information the detective had from the North Carolina authorities confirmed that it was indeed my son's body that had been found. Now what?

Amid my confused and shocked state of mind, the million questions that remain unanswered three years later, tears, a houseful of people, and more, I declared with confidence I was going to praise my way through this; it was not going to steal my joy, my mind, nor my peace.

Every time I think about making those statements within a few hours of knowing my child's body was lying in a morgue five hours away, I have no doubt it was the Spirit of God preparing me for what was to take place henceforth. Nine grueling days after we received the devastating news, we were finally able to funeralize our beloved son, Daniel, on Tuesday, August 13, 2019. It was the second worst day of my life.

Daniel's financial records revealed that he took a Lyft ride from his home to the Greyhound bus station in Richmond, Virginia, on the morning of Monday, July 29, 2019. No one ever came forth stating that they actually had any contact with him. He did not respond to any phone calls, text messages, or emails during that week. Further review of his financial and cell phone records indicated that Daniel traveled to Raleigh, North Carolina, via bus before continuing his travels via bus to Charlotte, North Carolina, where he arrived during the early morning hours on Saturday, August 3. It was more than sixty days after Daniel's death that the medical examiner's official report was received confirming that my beloved son died by suicide.

Now what?

The declaration I made on the night of his death was still looming in the recesses of my mind. But how? How could this complicated, devastating, gut-wrenching, and unexplainable demise of my child not steal my joy, my mind, and my peace? How does one praise their way through such a thing?

Meandering my way through the next six months was not easy. There was paperwork to manage, phone calls to make and take, insurance companies to deal with, road trips back and forth between Richmond and Newport News, and a whole lot more. Then came month seven, the day before what would have been Daniel's thirty-first birthday.

Seven months after Daniel's death, on Sunday, March 15, 2020, I was sitting on the bed in our hotel room in Virginia Beach, Virginia, reading and having some quiet time while waiting for Keith to finish dressing for the day. We would be joining two of Daniel's closest friends, Aaron and Lance, later that morning to celebrate Daniel's memory on what would have been his birthday weekend. Daniel and I had planned to do indoor skydiving at iFLY Virginia Beach. Daniel died before we had the opportunity to do so, but Lance agreed to do it with me in Daniel's memory. The COVID-19 virus had presented itself to the world just days prior. Businesses were shutting down because of it; fortunately, iFLY was able to remain open for business. Lance and I completed our jump before the four of us enjoyed lunch together at BJ's Restaurant.

While sitting on the bed, the thought dropped into my spirit that though the grief behind my son's death would be forever imbedded in my life, I was not going to allow it to consume me. Not only was I not going to be consumed by it, I was going to thrive in its aftermath!

One thing I have been sure about for a long time is my God-designed purpose to care for, encourage, and inspire women and support them when they get stuck or feel alone trying to determine what it is God has purposed for them. I have not always had clarity on how to fulfill my purpose, which causes me at times to question if I have gotten it right. The how, the where, and the who have taken on different shapes over the years, but always come back to showing empathy and compassion while nudging them to look to God, to listen to God, and to act accordingly. Surely the death of my beloved son would in no way be a part of it—or would it? How would I be able to serve anyone else while trying to figure out how to navigate through this unknown territory?

As I began to come to grips with the aftermath of Daniel's death and how it was not going to consume me, I had an epiphany. If this was my mantra, surely there must be others who had the same determination. Maybe, just maybe, my loss could in some way be used to care for, encourage, inspire, and support others who had a similar experience. I began to do some brainstorming, reading books about others' stories, researching on the internet and making plans for what I felt led to do.

My plans were waylaid from May to September 2020 while I dealt with a personal health challenge: stage 0 breast cancer. Really? Yes, really. I did not know until I knew that there was a stage 0. After numerous biopsies, surgeries, radiation, and the like, I would finally get back to actively making plans for how to move this grief train along; how to support others who were navigating grief just as I was.

But wait. Not so fast. Can you envision me glancing over my shoulder with a what-now look on my face? You envisioned correctly except it was not over my shoulder, it was muttered under my breath. When I noticed some shortness of breath and windedness while doing activities of daily living, I knew something was awry in my body. Tests ruled out scar tissue from the radiation and the formation of blood clots in my lungs, but the problem remained. Though I experienced it in my breathing, attention was turned to the neck area. The culprit turned out to be a goiter on the left side of my thyroid gland growing inward and pressing on my windpipe, thus the breathing issues. In May 2021, a total thyroidectomy alleviated the breathing problem, but other challenges with my overall wellness surfaced because of the surgery.

Still determined not to be consumed with grief while managing my health-related challenges, I forged ahead. I did what I could when I could with what I had available to me. I viewed the health challenges as a part of my purpose for the appointed time. Having to slow down enabled me to recognize I needed to do more work on myself before launching out to help others. I became acutely aware that if I was going to truly thrive in the aftermath, there were some things I needed to do. This is probably a good place to say some days grief won—and some days grief still wins. While I choose to live a positive lifestyle and tend to be a Pollyanna does not mean I do not have down days. There are days when I spend time vacillating between fantasy and reality about the death of my son. In fantasy mode, I do not have to remember that my son will never walk through my door again, I will never hear him say "Hey, Ma" again, or ever get to have another adventure with him, which is what we called our outings. I have chosen to give those times and days their space but do not allow them to consume me. I knew the effects of grief could be detrimental, so I would do everything in my power to not allow it to take my life captive. By now I knew there was a greater purpose to fulfill; one far greater than me succumbing to grief as a survivor of suicide loss.

I am hopeful that wherever you are on your journey in life, you will be able to glean something beneficial from the things I did and continue to do to thrive in the aftermath of the worst thing that has happened to me.

My Holistic Wellness Became My Priority

Taking exceptional care of myself became a priority after my son's death. My health challenge the following year heightened my desire to do so. I embraced self-love and self-compassion because if I was going to thrive in the aftermath, I had to go all in. If this experience was going to be a part of my plan to fulfill what I believed to be my God-ordained purpose, I had to go all in. Self-love and self-compassion are not looked upon favorably in some arenas, but I see them as being necessary unless it is done in a selfish manner. There is truth to not being able to pour from an empty vessel. Self-love and self-compassion are the best way I know how to show that I appreciate how God has blessed me—it is a part of how I take care of myself so I can fulfill the purpose He designed for me, which in turn will bring Him glory. A few things I do to help me keep my holistic wellness a priority are:

- Meet regularly with a paid friend (therapist).
- Challenge myself to do things I have never done.
- Engage with coaches and mentors for my multifaceted life.
- Bookend my days with a routine.
- Keep regular dates with myself.
- Practice mindfulness.
- Practice appreciation.
- Give myself grace.

Facing the Discomfort of Talking About My Loss

Grief is a bully! It will try to hold you hostage to the point of thinking no one cares, no one wants to hear it, no one else is going through it. When suicide is involved, an extra layer of emotions is added to the picture. In efforts to protect Daniel's character for the first year, I would say he *presumably* died by suicide. I was reminded at a conference my story could be someone else's painkiller and reason to move forward with their own loss regardless of what it was. I could no longer fear what others may say about me nor about my son and what he did. In my mind, it was a huge risk, but one that I finally decided was worth taking if I was going to fulfill my purpose and remain true to my declaration. The following are some things that help me face the discomfort of talking about my loss:

Created several one-hour talks that I host via ZOOM and in person.

S.H.A.R.E.E. (shock, hurt, anger, regret, escape, embrace) is about dealing with the emotions associated with grief and some ways to embrace them while moving forward.

S.T.I.N.G. (stop, turn, ignite, nurture, grow) the Stigma deals with the stigma surrounding suicide grief and how to manage it.

GRIEF—What's Time Got to Do with It? is about grief having no expiration date.

Pursued opportunities to talk about my loss.

Guesting on radio talk shows and podcasts has inspired me to continue talking about my loss. Serving as a guest speaker at events has proven to be helpful to me and to others. I have also submitted my story to some publications.

Created **TeaTime Chats with Lynn.**

TeaTime Chats with Lynn is a safe, non-clinical space for grieving women who are stuck and feeling alone with their loss to meet and support other women with similar experiences.

Sought out ways to honor my son's memory.

Volunteering with and supporting Full Circle Grief Center, participating in walks that bring awareness to mental wellness and suicide awareness, and making monetary donations to entities that were meaningful to my son are a few of the ways I honor his memory.

Invested in personal development.

Personal development is one of my life's core values. Research led me to grief coaching (not counseling), which I did not know existed. I embarked upon and completed the From Grief to Gratitude Grief Coaching Course. As a certified grief coach, I support my clients by guiding them from heartbreak to happiness, pain to peace, and grief to gratitude in the shortest time possible, but on their own terms.

I am also a student of others by intentionally engaging in conversations to learn and grow from their experiences. My story is just my story. If I am going to support people with stories different from mine, then it behooves me to be aware and learn about different experiences. I have found it to be some of the best education.

I often think about the declaration I made on that dreadful Sunday night, August 4, 2019. As a reminder, it was that I would praise my way through the complicated, devastating, gut-wrenching, unexplainable demise of my son. I would not allow it to take my joy, my mind, or my peace. Fast forward to now, just past three years later, through a myriad of difficulties, lessons learned, and lessons failed, and several other experiences, I am humble and grateful that I am thriving—not merely surviving—in the aftermath of his death. Humble that though I did not choose this burden, I get to be the one to help others find hope in their situations. Grateful that God has sustained me and entrusted the vulnerability of others to me and mine to them.

Thriving in the aftermath of the suicide death of my one and only child—my beloved son, Daniel—is a daunting experience; nevertheless, one I am determined to live out for the rest of my earthly days. I am grateful for the wonderful memories he left that help me navigate the grief jungle and thrive in its aftermath.

As I am writing this last sentence, I am praying that you will leave this story encouraged, inspired, and hopeful that you, too, can thrive in the aftermath of whatever your life's plight might be. Shalom!

Lynn Lewis

Lynn Lewis, a certified grief coach, loves that she gets to collaborate with adult women grieving the death of a loved one. They are women who have acknowledged and accepted that grief will forever be a part of their lives, but they desire to move forward living meaningful and impactful lives. She encourages, guides, and supports them as they make strides to move from heartbreak to happiness, pain to peace, and grief to gratitude.

There are few things Lynn finds more rewarding than joining a friend, colleague, or someone she has just met for a cup of tea and a chat. She never imagined those chats would involve sharing her grief story.

She has volunteered with several nonprofit organizations over the past twenty years, most recently with Circles RVA, Full Circle Grief Center, and Feed More. Lynn is happily retired from the automobile insurance claims industry; she resides in Richmond, Virginia, with her husband, Keith.

Contact her @ destinedtothrive@outlook.com
or connect with her on twitter.com/lynninspires and Facebook/Destined To Thrive Grief Coaching Services

Every Strand Counts

DANA WILSON

"Ma'am, unfortunately, your son will probably not make it through the night," the intensive care doctor said, gently touching my arm. My body felt numb as he continued to speak. "What's left of his intestines are swelling and applying pressure to his other organs, and that pressure could cause organ failure. In fact, if your son does survive, there's a strong probability that he will be brain dead."

The doctor's voice droned on. "You could relieve him of this pain and the uncertainty of his future by removing him from life support. You have a very difficult decision to make."

Lord, this must be a dream or a bad joke…Did that doctor just tell me I have only moments left to be with my five-month-old son, Landon?

As I sat in the chair, my thoughts returned to April 3, 2007, when Landon was born prematurely at twenty-four weeks, weighing in at only one pound, twelve ounces.

As I jumped up to go spend precious time with my baby, I was hailed by a voice. I turned to see Dr. Fischer, an Army surgeon who so happened to be working at the Children's National Medical Center, a civilian hospital, during a fellowship.

"Sergeant, what is the problem?" Dr. Fischer asked.

"Dr. Fischer," I said, "the medical team said the swelling in Landon's body is applying too much pressure on his other organs."

"Pressure, huh?" Dr. Fischer said. "I can relieve that."

He went directly to my son's intensive care unit bed and closed the curtain. Only minutes later, my son's intestines were hanging outside of his body encased in a plastic bag. He remained that way for several days under the eagle eye and vigilant care of Nurse Meg. She was determined that my son would not get an infection and that he would live.

September 10, 2007, altered the trajectory of my life. After my son's birth, my life consisted of living and sleeping at the hospital, going to work, researching my son's medical condition, a seemingly interminable procession of phone calls with various medical professionals most of whom I previously never even knew existed. Then there were therapists, social services, and nursing agencies. I made occasional trips home to do laundry, then the cycle would begin again.

I was Exhausted.

My military career kept me grounded. My son's medical care was covered by my service, and the support I received from my leaders lessened the emotional and physical stress I was under. The financial stability afforded by receiving regular pay was a blessing, and I cannot imagine how I would have managed if I had needed to worry about how I was going to eat.

I was exhausted.

Things were moving so fast. Life-or-death decisions had to be made with a clear head and heart, and I did not have either. The only and most important clarity I possessed was that God loved me, and it would be Him alone to guide me through this crazy time.

I was exhausted.

But my hair was poppin'! LOL. That may seem inconsequential at such a time, but I did not look like what I was going through or how I felt, despite the chaos swirling around me. Otherwise, I am sure that they would have admitted me into the hospital, too.

I started my Sisterlocks hair journey in 2000, so when Landon was born, I already had seven years of enjoying the natural freedom of this lifestyle under my belt. Sisterlocks is a natural hair management system that works with your natural texture. Basically, they are small style-able locks that only need retightening maintenance every four to six weeks. I could get fancy with curls or be easy with a finger-combed style and still look professional and within military standards. I was living in natural freedom.

As a serviceman, physical fitness, deployments, and being ready at a moment's notice were a necessity, especially as a general's aide. A general officer in the Air Force in certain positions and ranks was afforded this benefit because it was essential to their readiness. The duties required being a household manager, chef, assistant, travel coordinator, housekeeper, preparing uniforms, clothes, et cetera. You learn very quickly the delicate balance between being personable and being professional since you spend so much time with the general and the general's family in their private space. You want them at ease with you in their home, secure about their privacy, yet taken care of regarding the needs being met with your presence. As you might imagine, this position requires serious time management, interpersonal skills, and attention to detail.

Every Strand Counts

I quickly discovered that those personal service qualities refined as a general's aide became strands that were relevant and interlocked with my Sisterlocks business. I had already learned to hone these skills as a

Sisterlocks consultant. In fact, I was so excited regarding the natural freedom I was experiencing with my Sisterlocks that I decided to take the consultant training class that same year—in 2000. Originally, it was out of sheer curiosity. I did not have any intention to start a business. But after taking the initial training, things just took on a life of their own.

I loved sharing my own Sisterlocks journey and how this hair care management system had changed my way of life. Previously, I had spent so much time and money on equipment and products trying to manage my hair with relaxers or wearing my hair loose and natural. My hair care created an ongoing daily dilemma that determined much of what I did and where I went. It was so limiting and required so much energy and preplanning.

With Sisterlocks, the natural freedom one could experience was not only that it was beautiful and easy to care for, but more importantly, the style saved time and money. My Sisterlocks system choice freed me and paired well with my busy life.

It gets better. I even went on to become a Sisterlocks trainer. Now, I was sharing my love, experience, and skills of Sisterlocks with others in a way that they could go off and build their own businesses. Wow!

Every strand counts

My life radically shifted with my son Landon's premature arrival along with his severe life-threatening medical issues. I see now how my Air Force career in personal service and Sisterlocks training prepared me well to care for Landon.

Landon's medical needs required 24/7, around-the-clock care, which meant that in-home nursing care was a necessity. I was determined to find the right nurse, especially since we would need care during sleeping hours. Just as my general's aide role had taught me to serve, I required someone who could balance professional and personal simultaneously. I was experiencing both sides of the coin, as I was responsible for creating a good and comfortable working environment for my military leaders, now I needed to create the same in my own home.

Amid the mayhem, I sure did love my hair! My Sisterlocks gave me the freedom to roll with the punches. My life was so busy enjoying motherhood, managing Landon's medical care and military responsibilities, which included serving the generals and staying physically fit. My Sisterlocks were one of my superpowers to juggle it all without looking a mess.

Every strand counts.

Landon, my miracle baby, was developing and growing beyond what was predicted for him. We discovered he was on the autism spectrum, so we learned consistent, repetitive modalities to support his development one step at a time, and his small wins flourished into great gains. The basic concept of this strategy was not foreign to me. Establishing and maintaining Sisterlocks is a long game. It takes consistent, repetitive practice over time to make a continual work of art.

Every strand counts.

"Sergeant Wilson, have you ever considered that your new lifestyle and military life no longer align?"

The doctor's proposition seemed unthinkable at the time, but he had hit the nail on the head.

Soon after that conversation, God would have it that I retired early from the military. I was then able to devote more time to Landon. My life's pace slowed a bit, and I was able to pay more attention to myself. The ramification of service-before-self mindset began to rise to the surface.

Now, remember my Sisterlocks lifestyle was the one constant that was never a concern. Until I noticed I was losing my hair. I did not see locks falling out—ever. Not on my pillow or in the shower. Instead, I was experiencing a hair density change. As a Sisterlocks consultant, how could I be losing hair? I maintained a healthy regimen—regular retightening, shampooing, and moisturizing on a consistent basis. Why was I losing my hair? I was confused and became self-conscious and fearful of losing all my hair.

After doing some research, I learned from a trichologist (hair loss specialist) that many factors contributed to my hair loss issues, like poor diet, vitamin deficiency, lack of sleep, and fibroids. My blessing of being a mother of an autistic son with medical challenges was a stress factor that was also affecting my hair health. Ultimately, I was diagnosed with Central Centrifugal Cicatricial Alopecia (CCCA), a form of scarring alopecia on the scalp that usually results in permanent hair loss. CCCA is the most common form of scarring hair loss seen in African American women.

The fear of losing my health and beauty was the driving motivation that forced me into action. I complied with the trichologist's recommendations for lifestyle changes and was consistent with a personalized scalp and hair regimen. I personally continue to fight for every hair strand, and I am happy to say I am winning.

My awareness became a passion that "Every Strand Counts" and led me to become a certified trichologist. As a Sisterlocks consultant, I experienced the artistry of hair; as a Sisterlocks trainer, I enjoyed sharing the knowledge and skill of a unique hair management system. Now as a certified trichologist, I am committed to serving as a hair advocate to educate, encourage, and empower others that you do not have to suffer in silence. There is support and hair growth treatments known and available.

Prepare for Purpose

I get it! I can clearly see it now. I am God's continual work of art. God has been continuously and simultaneously preparing me for my purpose. My purpose in each given season is building blocks to my entire life's purpose.

My mother, the original training instructor, was prepping me to have the temperament for the military training style. She was a true disciplinary. This lady was no-nonsense.

Excuses were not accepted and follow-through to the end of a task, goal, or mission was demanded. I was groomed. She did her part and then passed the baton to the military, which indoctrinated me with more discipline, service before self, attention to detail, and curated those interpersonal skills. The military's lifestyle encouraged learning, education, and community.

That allowed me to sashay my way right into the Sisterlocks world. I had the essentials needed to be an effective consultant and trainer. Boy, did that discipline and follow-through come in handy to conquer that first Sisterlocks establishment of more than four hundred locks.

Sisterlocks opened my eyes to unique beauty. Each client arrived with different hair types, head shapes, and motivations. I practiced personalizing my approach and technique to each of my client's needs.

Prepare for purpose.

As unprepared as I felt for motherhood, then specifically for a special needs child, I am equipped. At least that's what I say to myself to keep motivated. LOL.

Landon requires all of me—all that my mother poured into me, all the military instilled, and all the beauty in the differences Sisterlocks helps me to see. God knew all that I needed to be equipped with to be ready for my Sweety Pea, my Duty Duty, my Landon.

When I push the rewind button, I can see so much of this in my life. God allowed lessons, blessings, trials, detours, triumphs, and situations to prepare me for my purpose for that time in life. I am grateful and excited to see what he has for me as I walk eyes wide shut through this human curation process.

Prepare for purpose.

See, God has got all of us covered. God has plans for us all. I challenge you to look back over your life. I am certain you can see how you were built brick by brick, moment by moment, and year by year. Things do not occur by happenstance.

Now, let's be clear: We make choices that take us on detours and roundabouts, but God works it out on our behalf.

Psalms 32:8 reads, "I will instruct you and teach you in the way you should go; I will counsel you with my eye upon you."

Jeremiah 29:11 reads, "For I know the plans I have for you," declares the LORD, "plans to prosper you and not harm you, plans to give you hope and a future."

Romans 8:28 reminds, "And we know that for those who love God all things work together for good, for those who are called according to his purpose."

We cannot discredit everything we have experienced, endured, and conquered.

> There is a time for everything,
> and a season for every activity under the heavens:
> a time to be born and a time to die,
> a time to plant and a time to uproot,
> a time to kill and a time to heal,
> a time to tear down and a time to build,
> a time to weep and a time to laugh,
> a time to mourn and a time to dance,
> a time to scatter stones and a time to gather them,
> a time to embrace and a time to refrain from embracing,
> a time to search and a time to give up,
> a time to keep and a time to throw away,
> a time to tear and a time to mend,
> a time to be silent and a time to speak,
> a time to love and a time to hate,
> a time for war and a time for peace.
>
> -Ecclesiastes 3:1–8

Acknowledging and recognizing that we are being prepped for our purpose can relieve some stress about our current circumstance.

We can walk tall with knowing that every strand counts.

Dana Wilson

Dana Wilson is the director of Hair Cares, Inc. She began her Sisterlocks journey in 2000 and then shortly thereafter became a certified Sisterlocks consultant. Dana progressed within the Sisterlocks family to trainer, coach, and brand ambassador.

Dana specializes in supporting people who may suffer from hair loss, scalp disorders, and Sisterlocks consultants who desire to build their businesses and hone their skills. She operates through offering trichology and Sisterlocks coaching, classes, and services.

Her motto is *Every Strand Counts*.

Dana has experience in home-based, salon, and mobile service settings. She has been able to incorporate her Sisterlocks business however needed in her busy life.

Mothering a special needs son has shown to be one of her superpowers. She has developed the unique ability to make complicated concepts simple. This ability aids in coaching others through hair regeneration and to be successful consultants.

Dana is a certified trichologist with personal hair-loss experience. She truly understands every strand counts. She has invaluable information and perseverance to pass on to clients and hair practitioners.

In her background for added skills, Dana is a United States Air Force veteran, a certified Cold Capper (for hair protection against chemo/radiation damage), and a certified bio-medical research assistant as well, all helpful in her portfolio to serve others.

No More Running

DR. TABATHA M. W. SPURLOCK

The Setup

> "She is clothed with dignity and strength and she laughs without fear of the future."
> —Proverbs 31:25

As a child, I was the oldest of three raised in a single-family household. I had my first formal job as a teen employee with the YMCA in high school during summer break. By my senior year, I had also worked at a local grocery store, fast food restaurant, and in corporate America as a Cooperative Office Education (COE) student. It was during my senior year of high school that I had aspirations to continue employment within corporate America or with the federal government. In my business classes, I recall learning that those environments would lead to job security. It was a great motivator for a little girl growing up in the hood.

Those career aspirations were short-lived when I transitioned as a part-time youth development professional with a local Boys & Girls Club. I became fond of the children and their families while working in different communities. Within a few years, I took my career with youth to the next level as an education career switcher within the K–12 public school system. After my first year, I knew I had made the right career choice and was a committed educator. In addition to teaching, I became the head cheerleading coach and elective department chairman. It was one of the best decisions of my life. I quickly learned that educating and mentoring teenagers was quite the challenge yet a rewarding experience.

I wanted to save all of my disadvantaged students, but I knew that it was impossible. Many of them were latchkey kids from single-parent households to which I could relate firsthand. They were likely going to be first-generation college students like myself as well. Instead of feeling defeated by what I couldn't do, every day I decided to focus on what I could do and empower one and inspire many. Today, I am proud to have many former students who beat the odds and are successful parents, entrepreneurs, and working professionals. I know my upbringing of living in a low-income neighborhood as the oldest of three helped me to show empathy to the students and community and educational environments that needed me the most where I could make a difference in the lives of others.

While building my career as a lifelong educator, I met my husband. The irony is that he actually had a federal government job with the security I thought I would need one day. There was balance with him being in a stable position and me being able to be in a service-oriented position doing what I love best—serving others and giving back to my community.

In the beginning of our marriage, there was lots of excitement. We were living in our first home built from the ground up. I frequently hosted Sunday football gatherings with friends, birthday and anniversary outings with other couples, and we traveled two to three times a year with either friends or family. Life was good—until one day there was a shift. We were having a conversation, and my husband felt like one of us needed a six-figure income to advance to our next level. We made beyond six figures collectively but not individually. My husband, who only had a bachelor's degree by choice, quickly declined the opportunity to go back to school for a master's degree. Neither of us was in a position to move up in our careers without additional certifications, licenses, or degrees.

After exploring our limited options, I decided to take one for the team and returned to school for the last time. I spent the next ten years pursuing a doctorate degree that would ultimately cost just as much as we were seeking annually in income. Why would I do that? In hindsight, it made sense at the time. I'm glad I know otherwise now, but that's all we knew, and I was willing to do whatever I could to help elevate and support our family.

Have you ever been in a position to pursue a goal that was by chance—that wasn't a part of your original plan? If so, what did you do, and how did it turn out? I never thought I would pursue a doctoral degree, yet I did.

A few encouraging words to share with you based upon the aforementioned history are as follows:

1. Be the first, and break generational curses.
2. Embrace life and your God-given gifts.
3. Allow yourself to love and to be loved.
4. Take the risk. Go for it!

The Setback

> "For I know the plans I have for you," declares the Lord,
> "plans to prosper you and not to harm you, plans to give
> you hope and a future."
> —Jeremiah 29:11

I was accepted into a doctor of education program with a concentration in leadership and technology. I opted for an online program, although at a higher cost, to afford me a work/life balance. Attending online classes allowed me to continue working my full-time job and to be home in the evenings with my family. I was required to successfully pass more than sixty credit hours of courses, attend four residencies away from home, and write and defend a dissertation to fulfill graduation requirements. It was an extremely demanding program that required a high level of time management skills and perseverance. I accepted the challenge.

I did my best not to neglect my family or my financial obligations for our household. I had to get creative with my time daily. Instead of socializing with colleagues on my lunch breaks, I was at my desk reading articles and writing. During the week, I was in my home office most nights between 11:00 p.m. and 3:00 a.m. completing assignments only to be up by 6:30 a.m. to get ready for work. On the weekends, I was a traveling scholar.

The finish line was in sight after completing Year 2 residency for the four-year program when I learned that I was pregnant with my first and only child. Talk about an influx of emotions. Ready or not, it was time to level up. We were still pursuing the six-figure lifestyle, but another shift was pending. We decided to build our second home to accommodate our family's growth, and this new home would be our forever home. Our beautiful daughter, Kennedi Alyse, was born on my late grandmother's birthday, August 26. I continued to push through my coursework like a boss with a 4.0 grade point average.

Six months later, my husband discovered his own six-figure plan and launched a home-based business. It was the beginning of a consecutive eight-year roller coaster ride and my ABD (all but dissertation) status. Oh, did I mention that my financial aid was running low, and I would soon have to pay for my final courses out of pocket? It was time for the superwoman cape to come off. I couldn't continue to meet my academic deadlines. Overnight, the business pursuit had me checking out of my own goals and dreams for our family. It was time for an executive decision.

I agreed to put my degree on hold for an entire year to support my husband in any capacity needed. Primarily, I cared for the children (our daughter and my bonus child) while holding down a full-time job and assisting with the business on a part-time basis. I'm pleased to say that we met the goal of becoming six-figure income earners within one year. However, the money was being made, yet the household wasn't seeing it. Within three years, our forever home was headed into foreclosure, and both of our luxury vehicles were repossessed.

Life felt overwhelming. I was losing myself. I realized no one was coming to save me—not even my husband. For once in my life, I didn't have the answers, yet I had to figure them out. I was in survival mode, and the perceived support by the general public from what they saw on social media wasn't my reality. I was fighting battles left and right with my head barely above water. In the end, I chose peace. It's easy to say what you will and won't deal with in life until you're in a position to deal with said things. I chose to fight through the hurt, pain, betrayal, and disrespect one day at a time still honoring the vows I took before God with dignity and self-respect.

Do you believe bad things happen to good people? I'm a good person, and I admit that I too have wondered why I had to deal with some of the setbacks that I have in life. Was it my karma? Was it God's way of testing my strength and endurance? Was it an attack from a loved one who harmed others that got passed down to me? Who knows, but the setback party was just getting started.

On October 27, 2016, I was excited to serve as a volunteer reader to elementary children as a central office employee. I arrived at the elementary school, pulled into a parking space, and sat in my car for a few minutes to gather my thoughts and pray. I was ready to empower a group of young minds, but I never made it into the building. As I walked from my car in the maze-like parking lot, a fellow parent driving an SUV ran me over. Moments later, I was laying on the ground unable to move my legs without discomfort. My pantyhose were torn with blood exposed from visible scarring on both legs, my leather boots were scratched up on both feet, and

I was perplexed as to what had just happened. The police arrived minutes later, and I was rushed to the emergency room for my first ambulance experience in life.

A few days later at my orthopedic appointment, my doctor concluded I suffered a tibial plateau fracture, and surgery was required within two weeks. As he spoke, my heart dropped, and there were uncontrollable tears running down my face. I immediately felt like a failure to my daughter because this meant we would have to postpone a trip I had promised her a month prior. The mommy guilt was real and overwhelming.

As you, too, are dealing with setbacks in life, I share the following tips on bouncing back like a B.O.S.S.:

B: Break away from distractions. Distance yourself from any and everyone feeding negative energy or words into your spirit. Realize that some situations and relationships require boundaries.

O: Own your decisions. Stay true to your thoughts and feelings without caving into the pressures of others. You won't always make others happy, so learn how to say no and mean it.

S: Stop asking for permission trying to please others, and take back your power. Live your life unapologetically.

S: Show up for yourself. No one is coming to save you, so save yourself.

The Comeback

> "Success isn't about how much money you make.
> It's about the difference you make in people's lives."
> —Michelle Obama

I was able to return to work after three months, but something just didn't feel right. As I passed colleagues in the hall, on the elevator, and in the parking lot, the million-dollar question couldn't be avoided: "Are you okay?" And my accustomed response was "Yes, I'm okay," knowing I was on the verge of an emotional breakdown. I didn't recognize myself anymore. My colleagues didn't know it, but I would hide in my office most days with my door closed in avoidance of others. I didn't want or like all of the newfound attention, but there was one sweet lady whose desk was near the restroom who made me smile. She was more mature and had a way of making me feel good in my broken state.

By summer, I had cut my hair and became withdrawn from others, not feeling like the go-getter I was prior to the accident. Eventually, I was diagnosed with post-traumatic stress disorder, anxiety, and depression. I was suffering and didn't know what to do. Within a week of the diagnosis, I quit my dream job after only serving in that capacity for two years. It took me ten years, starting out as a classroom teacher, to earn the central office position, but I wasn't okay and didn't really know how to ask for help. As a strong friend and family member, some people left me to figure things out on my own while others saw through my attempts of isolation. *How do I cope and survive?* was the main thing on my mind. Since the system wasn't willing to give me the support I needed, I was forced to put my own self-care plan in place.

If you have never encountered a major setback in life, count your blessings. I hate to be the bearer of bad news, but life happens to all of us. It can be a stressful and overwhelming ordeal, especially if you're without a strong support system. Lean on your faith knowing that God makes no mistakes. If He brought you to it, then He will bring you through it.

On top of the accident recovery and no full-time job, my family was in the midst of a foreclosure and downsizing to an apartment on the other side of town. I was teaching part-time as an adjunct professor at a local HBCU (historically black college and university) and had to fight back tears and emotions daily to put on a brave face for my students and colleagues from the moment I left my car. God positioned me to fulfill my passion and purpose in life right before the chaos to keep me grounded and focused. Hell was breaking loose in other areas of my life as well. I had to tell myself, "You may not understand it now—the pressures of life may seem too hard to bear—but you will survive and make it on the other side in the end."

I volunteered to speak to a group of first graders on the day my life changed forever, and today I'm a best-selling children's book author. My book, *A Promise Is a Promise*, is in every state in the United States, Canada, and the United Kingdom. It is in school libraries, and I've had the pleasure of being a guest author reading my book to children, families, and staff. I never in my wildest dreams envisioned being a children's book author. God has a funny way of redirecting or directing our lives. I stopped counting at one thousand sales, and I appreciate my story reaching families who are dealing with guilt and empty promises—a delay is not a denial. He was preparing me for my purpose before I knew it.

A few things to remember during your comeback season:

- Give yourself some grace if you are a parent. I was beating myself up at times because our daughter had to switch schools. She adjusted fine and has more friends and teachers she's positively affected than I can keep up with most days.
- Go to therapy or counseling and take your family with you. My therapist was the one who reassured me that the change with our residence was a good thing.
- Be comfortable with changing your environment. A change of scenery and living conditions brought about peace from the constant reminder of the accident.
- Be secure in who you are because people will try to project their own insecurities on you. Do not let them.
- Pray. I know God got tired of me asking Him, "Why me? Why did you put me in that place at that time for my life to be changed forever?" His reply: "Jeremiah 29:11." He knew that I wouldn't

sit on my story. He knew when I didn't even know how I would overcome that traumatic situation. He knew that my own healing journey would lead to healing for others. Every time I tell my story, I can't help but give God all of the glory for where I am today.

- Secure a safe space in your home that brings you peace and allows you to release.
- Designate time daily or weekly to journal.
- In the midst of it all, don't lose your smile. It doesn't mean that you're not hurting. It just means that you desire to become better and not bitter as you fight through the pain.

Conclusion

Two months prior to the 2020 global pandemic, I returned to the classroom. I didn't ask God for a career advancement opportunity. I needed health benefits and asked for an opportunity that would help me get back on track as an educational leader and one that allowed me to exude my passion.

As I bring my chapter to a close, others often say to me, "You don't look like what you've been through" after hearing my story. I would say that is a true statement. When I think about all that the Lord has brought me through, I can't help but smile and be grateful. My new personal motto is "My life is not my own." My gifts are meant to be shared with others, including my story, and I hope you will join me on this "no more running" journey.

Finish that degree…I did. Buy the car…I did. Take the trip…I did. Build the business and write the book…I did—and went bestseller multiple times. Never in a million years did I see myself as a teacher. However, I have learned that our purpose in life can change based upon our personal desires and life events. You owe it to yourself to live a fulfilling life on purpose with a purpose. Take ownership of the spaces you occupy with no regrets.

Dr. Tabatha Spurlock

Dr. Tabatha Spurlock is a wife, mother, entrepreneur, serial bestselling author, philanthropist, highly energetic motivational speaker, and educator for nearly twenty years. She volunteers with several community organizations and enjoys serving as a mentor and board member for a nonprofit organization called MEGA Mentors. This leader has a true servant's heart and desire to help uplift, motivate, and inspire others.

In 2016, she was the victim of a traumatic accident that left her unable to walk unassisted for three months. Over the years, she's had to learn how to conquer her diagnosis of post-traumatic stress disorder, anxiety, and depression. While the journey has been extremely challenging at times, she has learned how to bounce back from life's setbacks with ease. She is no longer running from the trauma and pain. She's using her voice to help inspire and empower others.

Directing Your Path to Purpose

CHANDRA BROADNAX-PAYNE

"And we know that in all things God works for the good of those who love him, who have been called according to his purpose. For those God foreknew, He also predestined to be conformed to the image of his Son, that He might be the firstborn among many brothers and sisters. And those He predestined, He also called; those He called, He also justified; those He justified, He also glorified." —Romans 8:28–30

I can still remember like it was yesterday. The time was in the 1970s in Brooklyn, New York—the projects of East New York. My mom would put on her favorite gospel music or rhythm and blues. As we listened to the likes of The Isley Brothers or James Cleveland, my mother would pull out one of her favorite books and unwind all weekend and slip into another world. I remember watching her with such intensity as only a loving little daughter would do. I decided that I too would grow up and read a lot of books. That excitement about books would later turn into a passion for stories and my desire to write my own books and films.

I truly believe that one only has to go back to their childhood to catch a glimpse of their purpose and their future. At the tender age of three, I had a pencil in hand and paper regularly. Let my mom tell it, my writings ended up on the apartment walls, paper, dressers, and anything within my reach.

By the time I could speak well enough, I entertained my mom and sister regularly with stories of my imaginary friend Peppa who was a scrappy little British girl who always seemed to make her way into the most mischievous moments of my life. Thank goodness for growth, as I no longer blame Peppa for my wrongdoings. As I entered my preteen years, I began writing poetry about love and racism. By the time I was fourteen, I became a published poet. As I look back over my life, I can see that all of these things would later become clues to my purpose.

God would continue to leave subtle clues and give me a glimpse into my purpose as the years continued. As a student of PS 273 in East New York, my favorite part of the day was spent in Mrs. Giovanni's class. Growing up in the projects to a single mother in the era of the crack epidemic left most children my age scared of daily violence. But thank God for Mrs. Giovanni. While my friends and I ducked under kitchen tables and walked the dangerous blocks and hallways of our apartment buildings, Mrs. Giovanni showed us a glimpse of what the world outside of our projects looked like. Every day during recess, we were given the opportunity to lay our heads down on our desk as she would play classical music for an hour. While most kids rested, I would close my eyes and listen to the unique music playing over the room, and I would dream about life and my future. I would use that time to draw out my ideas for music videos. One of my dream jobs back then was to become a music video director. I remember the first music video treatment I did was for Puff Daddy's "Don't Stop What You're Doing."

Long after I left PS 273, I found myself listening to classical music, and

R&B while writing poems. Later on, the poetry turned into short stories and the desire to enter the film industry. I would stand in front of my bedroom mirror and pretend that I was being interviewed on the red carpet or by a media outlet. As a child, I would practice how I would answer questions about my films. A few years ago, I had my first media interview about my documentary *A Silent Enemy*. Those practice interviews as a child were no coincidence. They would later prepare me as filmmaker for interview in print, ABC, and CBS, as well as radio outlets and twenty-two podcasts in the span of one year.

Fast forward to undergraduate graduation. One of my peers stopped me in the student commons to ask what I was planning to do after I graduated, to which I replied so quickly, "I'm going to save lives through my words." The words flew out of my mouth so fast they startled me. I had no idea why I said those words, what they meant, or even why I said them with such authority and confidence.

After graduating from undergrad, I landed a job in corporate America. Over the next few years, I would work in various fields such as employee engagement and management. The first few years of my career, I was so excited to have graduated and have some money in my pocket to pay off some bills and get my first apartment. After a few years though, the excitement of the nine to five started to wear off. I began to think about my first love of writing and film. Despite the promotions and visibility within my organization, there was a small part of me that wished I could live out my dreams. Can you imagine waking up every day of your life knowing that there is something else you were called to do? It felt like I had a hole in my heart; there was a piece of my life that was missing daily. I knew that I had to make a change in order for the hole to mend.

After years of running from the calling on my life, God saw fit that I could no longer run. Fear nor a busy work schedule could no longer keep me from doing what I was destined to do. After sustaining a neck injury that left me bedridden for almost a year, I decided to take out my pen and paper. It started with daily journal writings about my life and how

I overcame depression. I remember very vividly laying on my back and holding the journal up in the air and writing until my arms were tired. I did this for several months until I heard God say, *You thought these journal writings were just for you, but they're not. This will become your first book. Your pain, all your trials, and the depression will be used to save others who are going through pain and trials.*

Can I tell you how reluctant I was at first? To the outside world, I appeared to live a good life, but on the inside, I was hurting. But I knew that I had to heed God's instruction, so I did just that. In 2018, I would publish my first book, *You Go Girl: 25 Ways to Step into Your Greatness*. A nod to all my sisters out there who have ever faced challenges in life. After bouncing back from depression, I promised God I would share my message and let others know they don't have to be ashamed of their journey—that it is possible to get back up again. It would take many years before I would connect the dots.

Flashback to the student commons. I told my peer I was going to save lives through my words. Isn't God amazing? He gave me a glimpse of my future back then. I had no idea what that meant. But he gave me that and put it down in my spirit many years ago. Becoming an author gave me the courage to try my hand at my next leg of my purpose, and that was film.

In 2019, I began pre-production for my first feature-length film *A Silent Enemy*, about domestic violence. Are you seeing a pattern here? God gave me those words back in college, and many years later, I am doing just that. And by 2021, I had done my second film.

> "The purpose of life is a life of purpose."
> —Robert Byrne

What Is Purpose?

The word *purpose* has been used by many coaches, gurus, and leaders. According to dictionary.com, purpose is the reason for which something exists or is done, made, or used. Each one of us has a purpose. It is the reason we were created to manifest and live out what we were created to do.

Finding your purpose is a journey; it doesn't happen overnight. We are all constantly evolving and growing. The one thing I know is that we can try to avoid purpose, pretend it doesn't exist for us, but it does. Just when you least expect it, purpose will find you if you are open to the journey.

> For I know the plans I have for you," declares the Lord,
> "plans to prosper you and not to harm you, plans to give
> you hope and a future."
> —Jeremiah 29:11

If you haven't guessed by now, our purpose was already predetermined before you and I were born.

Your Purpose Isn't Just for You

As I sat on my bedroom floor suffering from depression and suicidal thoughts, I remember God spoke to me about sharing my story to help others who may be going through trials.

What has God spoken to you about your purpose? Are you living in your purpose? If you're not, are you fulfilled? I remember the many lessons I learned along the way and the trials and tribulations I had to face to get to my purpose. I remember asking, "Why am I going through all this suffering?" It was one day that it finally hit me that I couldn't speak to other women about depression and other trials if I had not gone through the depression and trials and tribulations. God used those situations in my life so that when I speak to other women and write about it, I am speaking from the heart—from experience. My experience qualified me for it. How could I be a good steward of the gifts the father has given me if I don't share what I've learned to help others?

You may not have gone through depression, but maybe your trial is your kids, your marriage, or something else. But there is something that you know, experienced, and feel deep down on the inside of you that God wants you to use for His glory and to bless others. Here are some tips that I have used in my own life to plan for purpose that I want to share with you.

1. Make sure you are connected to God.

2. Be obedient to the voice of God. Sometimes we keep ourselves busy doing things without waiting to hear from God.

3. Heed His instructions for your life. If God says go, then go. If He says not yet, then be still. Warning: Do not move forward unless you are given the green light to do so. Every time I've moved forward when He told me to be still, it ended in disaster.

While you are waiting to hear from God, make sure that you are doing the work to prepare for your purpose. For years, even before I became a published author, film director, or producer, I quietly did the work and educated myself about the film industry. Some people have asked how I started writing, and they think it's an overnight process, but it hasn't been. I went to acting workshops, read books, and networked with others in the industry. After all, how could I direct actors if I did not learn what I could about the craft? People often ask how to break into the industry. Here are a few key ways to enter into the industry:

1. **Enroll in film school.** There are many schools out there that are waiting to enroll you in one of their amazing film programs. When it comes to obtaining a film degree, there are many schools from New York to Los Angeles and in between that will provide you with a comprehensive overview of the film industry from the history of film, video production, writing, as well as the business of film.

2. **Pick up a camera.** While there are benefits to attending a film school, not everyone has the ability to do so—not everyone has the desire, the finances, or the time. For those of you who want to make films without a formal education, there is still hope. All you need is an idea, a plan, and a camera. You would be surprised at the number of films that have been done on an iPhone.

3. **Network, network, network, and network with those in the industry.** For those who desire to break into the industry, you no longer have to live in New York or Los Angeles to meet people in the industry. The internet has made it easier to meet people. You can search for groups and organizations within the industry and connect with the people in the groups.

4. **Learn the business.** There is more to what you see on the big screen. The global movie production and distribution industry estimated the global film production and distribution industry would amount to $76.7 billion by the end of 2022. The industry is a money-making machine. I guarantee you no matter how good a film idea is, if there isn't an audience for it, a studio will not pick it up. If a studio doesn't believe they can make money off the film, it won't be picked up. Some things you can look for are the types of films that are being made. Are there certain genres that are popular on the big screen right now? How much money are the films bringing in? A great place to start is with IMDB. This website lists a lot of useful information about the revenue of various films.

5. **Study films.** Watch films, and don't just stick to one genre. Watch many different types of films. What kinds of films interest you? What are the running times for the films? Study the actors, music, and even dialogue. Look for patterns in the films you are watching.

6. **Tell stories that matter to you.** The filmmaking process is very lengthy and sometimes painstaking yet rewarding. If you get into the industry haphazardly "just because," trust me, it will show in the quality of your work. Don't get into the industry because of ego. I have had many people tell me, "I just want my name to be in lights." Here is what I ask those people: Why? We have call times as early as 5:30 a.m. and work ten- to twelve-hour days, and that doesn't include the months and sometimes years of preparation. Trust me, this is not a business to get into because you think it's glamourous. It is rewarding, but it is a lot of work.

How to Plan for Your Purpose

You never know when it will be your moment to shine. That's why I live by the motto to stay ready because you never know when an opportunity will present itself for you to walk into your purpose. Earlier in the chapter, I spoke about the clues that life leaves into your purpose. Some of the clues for my purpose included writing music treatments for videos, writing poetry, short stories, and pretending to be interviewed by media outlets to name a few. It didn't make sense back then, but it all makes sense now. God was preparing me little by little so that when the time came for me to take the leap into my purpose, I was ready.

Take a few moments to think about some of the clues—those breadcrumbs—that are leading you into your purpose. I assure you that you will notice a pattern. There will be small little clues that all add up to your purpose. As you are preparing and walking along this journey, remember to get ready, prepare, educate yourself on the topic you are interested in; network; and practice, practice, and practice.

What are three things that you can do to plan for your purpose? Maybe you aren't the next budding filmmaker. You might be the next chief executive officer of the healthcare industry or the next TEDx speaker.

What steps could you take now while you are on your journey?

1

2

3

See you at the top.

Chandra Broadnax-Payne

Author, filmmaker, philanthropist, film director, and executive producer Chandra Broadnax-Payne is a native of Brooklyn, New York, but now calls North Carolina home. The North Carolina-based filmmaker is known for her truth-seeking curiosity and creativity. Broadnax-Payne enjoys telling stories and bringing awareness to projects that highlight issues within society that are often not addressed or overlooked. Her film *A Silent Enemy* is a feature-length documentary about domestic violence in the African-American community and the silence that perpetuates it. The documentary has received many accolades and has even gained the attention of numerous media outlets and distributors from Los Angeles to New York. She has been featured on ABC, CBS, AND 101.3 as well as several print publications.

Her films have played at several festivals including Afrikana Independent Film Festival, NC Black Film Festival and Heritage Film Festival.

She is a graduate of Virginia Commonwealth University where she received a degree in mass communications. Broadnax-Payne believes in the power of education and, as a result, has gifted ten scholarships to ten minority women over the past ten years.

When she is not working on a film, she enjoys spending time with her husband and giving back to her community.

Visit her website at www.asilentenemy.com
or connect with her on instagram.com/asilentenemy and instagram.com/chandrabpayne or facebook.com/asilentenemy

Processed for a Purpose

DESIREÉ HARRIS-BONNER

"In the beginning God (Elohim) created [by forming from nothing] the heavens and the earth. The earth was formless and void or a waste and emptiness, and darkness was upon the face of the deep [primeval ocean that covered the unformed earth]. The Spirit of God was moving (hovering, brooding) over the face of the waters. And God said, 'Let there be light'; and there was light. God saw that the light was good (pleasing, useful) and He affirmed and sustained it..." —Genesis 1:1–4a (AMP)

Throughout the entire first chapter of Genesis, one of the first things we learn about God is that He is exceptionally detailed—He took chaos and brought it into order—and that He does nothing just for the sake of doing it. Everything He does is intentionally taken through a process for a purpose. Therefore, should we truly desire to prepare ourselves for purpose, we must also understand and embody this aspect of His nature. So, let's lean into that a bit.

A Lesson from David

I love to read, and since many of the most compelling and impactful stories can be found in the Bible, it only follows that I love reading them. I read the stories both for a glimpse into the heart and mind of our Father and to discover how I can apply these to my life, relationships, and business in this present climate…viewing its content not so much singularly in terms of each verse but as a whole in the context of the lessons and practical applications contained within.

Aside from the creation story in the book of Genesis, one that has significantly impacted my understanding of being processed for a purpose is the biblical account of David's anointing by the Prophet Samuel to become the second king of Israel (1 Samuel 16).

Now, remember that at this time, David was still a boy in his late teens who spent his time in the mountains shepherding his father's sheep—not yet old enough to serve in the king's army, let alone be a king. So, when Samuel asked David's father, Jesse, to assemble his sons, Jesse produced all of them, except for one: David. He hadn't bothered calling him in from the field because surely, he was not the soon-to-be king.

Samuel, unaware that one of the eight sons was missing, proceeded to anoint each of Jesse's seven other sons. One by one, he attempted to pour the oil over their heads; however, the oil would not flow. There was no anointing for any of those present, even though they all appeared to be the perfect choice for a king.

I want to pause here to note the integrity of Samuel. He feared God and was so deeply committed to his role as a prophet he did not seek to save face when it looked to everyone as if he had made a mistake. He refused to pretend that the future king was among them, nor did he question himself or second-guess God. Samuel knew what God had told him to do, so he was aware that there had to be another explanation.

So, he questioned Jesse.

> Then Samuel said to Jesse, "Are all your sons here?" Jesse replied, "There is still one left, the youngest; he is tending the sheep." Samuel said to Jesse, "Send word and bring him; because we will not sit down [to eat the sacrificial meal] until he comes here."
>
> —1 Samuel 16:11

There it was. The oil wasn't pouring because *God had not chosen them for this purpose*. But, the part that stood out for me was that Samuel would not move forward until David had been invited. As David would later write, "he prepares a table before me..." (Psalm 23:5).

How often have you entered situations where others could not believe that anyone was choosing you for something big, special, or important? They couldn't possibly be talking about you because you did not seem to fit that particular purpose. But the truth is that He will make room for you whether or not others believe you belong there.

* * *

God will stop the whole show for you
when you are on purpose for a purpose.

* * *

In case you aren't familiar with the conclusion of that account, once David arrived, the oil of anointing flowed freely—an anointing that flowed for generations to come—all the way to Jesus Himself.

However, if you continue reading, you will quickly discover that this ruddy teenager didn't immediately pack his bags and head to the castle to reside as the king of Israel. It would be quite some time before that would happen. Unlike most of us who would have instantly thrown out our shepherd business cards and put in new ones that read *King of Israel*, David "went back and forth from Saul to tend his father's flock at Bethlehem" (1 Samuel 17:15).

Not only that, among other things, he would have to fight a Philistine giant, have spears chucked at him by the current king, and find himself hiding in caves before he would reign as God's chosen king over His people. In other words, David had to go through a process to be prepared for his purpose.

Lesson from Cindy

Another story that helped me understand the power of going through a process to be prepared for a purpose—one of my favorites to read as a kid—was the tale of Cinderella. That may sound odd considering the previous example, but stick with me. Be aware, however, that I'm not talking about the popular Disney version. Although similar in some parts, I'm referring to the grittier Brothers Grimm version. So, we'll pick up where the prince's messenger was sent out to find the one who had worn the shoe found on the castle steps after the third night of the ball.

> "It was so tiny that he was sure only the mysterious princess would wear it. When the stepsisters heard this, each one was sure she could somehow squeeze her foot into the slipper. A messenger was sent from house to house with the slipper, and all the young ladies tried to put it on. But they tried in vain, for it would not fit."
> —Ashenputtel, 1812

Like David in our biblical story earlier, Cinderella—or Cindy as I like to call her because we're cool like that—was not invited to the proceedings. Instead, she was relegated to the stony, cold kitchen while her stepmother brought out her stepsisters, and they both—first one and then the other—tried on the glass slipper. The girls tried so hard to push their feet into the dainty shoe that their bones cracked; one sister cut her toes off to make it fit, and the second chose to cut off her heel. The deception was only discovered as blood leaked from the sides of the shoe, pooling on the floor as they walked.

I told you it was different than the well-known kid version! Still, can you see the parallel to our earlier account of David? In our fairy tale, the stepmother, stepsisters, and probably the whole village could not fathom that Cindy might be the fair maiden who had danced with the prince until midnight, stealing his heart. The truth of who Cindy (and her purpose) was could be revealed only after coming out from where she had been hidden.

> "When purpose is not known, abuse is inevitable."
> — Myles Munroe; *Understanding the Purpose and Power of Woman*

We don't know what happened to Cindy once she had babies, stretch marks, mother-in-law issues, et cetera, because the story doesn't tell us that. It just says, "they lived happily ever after." For all we know, things might have been difficult for her polishing the shining armor of her knight. Nevertheless, as David became king and had his issues, Cindy became a princess. And so goes our story as we walk with God and follow His will. God's purpose for us will manifest itself.

Unfortunately, many of us have no idea that we are forcing ourselves into a role, position, or title that does not belong to us or that we are cutting off parts of ourselves to fit into something we were never designed for. We either try to function in a way that was not in His original plan for us, simply because it looks good or it's comfortable, or we allow others to keep us relegated to their opinions and ideas of who we are rather than who we were created to be.

God's will and plan for us is the round hole, and we morph ourselves into a square peg. Then we are confused as to why we struggle to actualize His purpose for our lives.

A Custom-Designed Purpose

One thing that perplexed me about David's story was that the oil would not pour from its vessel. I mean, gravity alone would force it to come down, right? And in Cindy's story, in all the land where she resided, there was no other person or woman who wore the identical size shoe as her? The story takes great pains to tell us that all the maidens in the land had tried on the slipper, yet only she could fit into it.

It took me a few years, but then I understood. Whether literal or figurative, the anointing was for David alone. The oil was specific to his purpose and could not be attached or attracted to anyone else. And the glass slipper had been formed for Cindy alone. No one else could walk in it.

* * *

Both David and Cinderella had a purpose that was designed specifically for them.

* * *

I'll give you an example of a situation in the past with my baby sister. One day, I bought these gorgeous shoes. We called them "cold-blooded" back then. Today, we might say that they were "fiyahh!" Anyway, they were four-inch stiletto sandals in my favorite color, black, with straps that came up to the knee. I was thrilled to bring them home. But before I had a chance to wear them, baby sis asked for them, insisting they would look great with her outfit for that night. Of course, I loaned them to her, and she proceeded to "borrow" them for the next few months. However, when she brought them back, I couldn't wear them. They were still a size nine, a medium, and fit my foot, but I couldn't wear them.

Why not? Because of the way sissy is built. Due to her being slightly bow-legged, my sister has a different way of walking, a different way of standing—a different wear pattern. I didn't walk the way she did. I didn't stand like her, so when I tried to walk in them, they naturally bent to the outside. They were my shoes, but they no longer "fit" me—but perfectly fit her…the way she is. And yes, I gave them to her.

Since then, I have learned that there are three components to a custom-designed purpose: *size*, *fit*, and *wear*.

> **Size is what you do in your life.** Let's say my shoe size is a nine, meaning that the length of my foot is a U.S. woman's nine. That's the length of that shoe, as well as my foot. Using the analogy of the business world, perhaps I am a coach. My size could be coaching. If you put me in most coaching positions, I will do well, as I have the skill, education, and experience needed.

> **Fit is the way you fill out what you do.** It is more about the breadth and reach of your skills, gifts, and talents, referring to the width of the shoe, not the length—what we might call your "niche." So, I am a nine in size, but I am a medium fit, as opposed to a narrow or wide. Using our business analogy, if my size is being a coach, my width is how I fit into the coaching space. I might be a business coach, a life coach, a health and wellness coach, or a personal trainer. I might work with a particular demographic or focus on a specific community. And I might be entrepreneurial, work for a small business, or be employed within a corporate or governmental structure.

Most people stop at size and fit. But what made the difference for David and Cindy went beyond those two components. It is not only what you do or how you fill the space of what you do. The third component, which I will expound on below, is what makes our purpose a custom-designed one.

> **Wear is how you do what you do.** It has everything to do with all of the elements and components you bring to the table—all aspects of who you are: your personality, your experiences, your relationship

with God, your level of communication with Him, the processes and refinement that you have gone through. To follow the coaching metaphor, wear is that which differentiates you and sets you apart from all other coaches. It is your personal style and story—the way you walk in it. Much like how my sister and I wore the same size shoe, how she wore it made it so that it no longer fit me; it only fit her. It includes everything that makes you uniquely you so that only you can wear that shoe the way that you do.

* * *

No one can do what you do...
the way you do what you do!

* * *

So, what can we take away from David's and Cindy's stories? For me, it is the knowledge that when God breathed into each of us the breath of life and made us living beings (Genesis 2:7), He was saying, "I have custom-designed a purpose for you that you genuinely fit into."

In that life-giving breath was the "Spirit" that contained the virtues, gifts, and anointing needed to accomplish His purpose for us, which has always been within us like seeds planted in the ground that require watering, waiting to be increased. Meaning that we don't have to do anything to find our purpose; it is already in us—we simply need to be prepared for it when it presents itself.

Again, our Daddy is a God of order... He is able to take everything we do (both good and not so good) and use it to process us into our purpose. The key is that we remain connected to His Spirit, the Paraclete, the One called alongside us to help.

> "A man's gift [given in love or courtesy] makes room
> for him, And brings him before great men."
> —Proverbs 18:16 (AMP)

Developing Your Story

Having said all of that, this is what I want you to do over the next few days: Sit with Daddy and get quiet. Open your heart and allow Him to speak to you about the "shoes" you have been wearing. It doesn't matter if you have been wearing a size nine for the past fifty years. Maybe they hurt your feet because they are someone else's. Maybe they are too narrow. Maybe you're in the wrong shoe wearing the wrong size. With pen and paper in hand, ask Him these three questions:

- What is my size—what is it that I am called to do?
- What is my fit? How do I fill that space? What is my niche, specificity, or specialty?
- What unique capabilities and skillsets do I bring that You want me to utilize so that I can do it my way—the way you have gifted and designed me?

I don't know anyone who has tried this exercise and failed to get an answer. However, it may not come as a thunderclap from the sky. Most times, it comes as a still, small voice or as one believer said, "A knowing in my knower." It is a space where peace resides.

If He says, "Daughter, you wear an 8.5 medium; it fits you better," be ready to listen and pivot. A commitment to your custom-designed purpose releases the oil so that the anointing can fall and flow through your being, and you will be fully prepared for your purpose.

> "God saw everything that He had made, and behold,
> it was very good and He validated it completely."
> —Genesis 1:31 (AMP)

Desireé Harris-Bonner

Elder Desireé Harris-Bonner is the founder and managing partner of her global firm, DHBonner Virtual Solutions, LLC, where she operates as a spiritual midwife for emerging authors by providing ghostwriting, editing, author coaching, and book creation and design support to international businesses, worldwide ministries, and independent solopreneurs.

With more than thirty years of experience working for Fortune 20 corporations, Desireé holds a bachelor's degree in organizational leadership and a master's degree in business. As an ordained elder, she has an extensive history supporting and mentoring aspiring bus-inistry owners to thrive in partnership with God while having a greater impact in both the Kingdom and the Marketplace.

Having spent her childhood as a GI brat who has lived all over the world, she currently makes her home in Central Florida. Her greatest loves are her three adult children and six grandchildren.

For booking or more information,
visit her website at www.dhbonner.net

Positioned for Purpose

JOICE M. SAWYER

Have you ever asked yourself, "Why am I still living?" especially after the last unprecedented two years we have seen? We were on lockdown; could not go to a mall, to school, to work, or church because the government prohibited us from doing so due to a deadly virus called COVID-19. It took the lives of so many people. For some of us, COVID took the lives of our mothers, fathers, sisters, brothers, husbands, wives, dear friends, and loved ones, and we were not allowed to sit by their bedside to support in their time of need. I mean every day you woke up and the phone rang, despite how much faith you had, you wondered who would be next. For some of us who contracted the deadly virus, sometimes we felt it was impossible to breathe, and we wondered, Is this it?

Yet and still, if you are reading this book, you are still here. Why? Out of all the people who left this earth in the last two years, why do you still exist? May I submit to you, you exist because you have purpose. Every one of us is alive because we have purpose. Everything and everyone has purpose. We were created for purpose. It is the reason we exist. If we do not fulfill our purpose, we will be unsuccessful in life.

Let us take for example an automobile. It has purpose. The automobile's purpose is to transport, and if for some reason, the automobile fails to transport, it is unsuccessful. The automobile has not fulfilled its purpose, and so it is in our lives, if we fail to fulfill the reason we were created. If we fail to use our gifts and talents, our lives will never be fulfilled. We stop the flow and the influence of our lives and others'.

It does not matter what your title is—whether it is doctor, lawyer, mother, schoolteacher, police officer, janitor, professional football player, professional basketball player, nurse, caretaker, or wife, we all have purpose.

Purpose is the reason for which something is done or created or for which something exists. It has an objective and a goal to strive toward something that already exists. It is when we put our intentions, desires, and our determinations all together with our God-given talents and gifts. There's not a person here on earth who does not have purpose. When things happen in our lives, it seems like our purpose has been derailed, distorted, or sabotaged. This zaps our morale and causes us to want to abandon our God-given purpose.

Romans 8:28 says, "And we know that all things work together for good to those who love God, to those who are called according to His purpose." Some situations, events, and even people have been placed in our lives by design. And to God, a design is just that. It is a drawing of what is to come—a blueprint, a motif, a plan of what is to come. What He has designed for our life cannot be thwarted by anything life brings. We must understand that God will use loss, betrayal, trials, and persecution to push or propel us into purpose. While going through, we think He is allowing these things to destroy us, but in fact He is pushing us, aligning us, developing us into purpose. Life's struggles prepare us for purpose. No matter how much we've lost or how many times we have failed and missed the mark, purpose finds a way to get back up again.

Every closed door is not a bad thing. Every person who walks away is not a mistake. Some of us need a push. When everything is comfortable, we remain where we are because it is comfortable. We do not like being uncomfortable. We do not like change. We do not like being stretched. Purpose can be lonely. Purpose can cause you to sever relational ties. Purpose will cause you to be isolated. Purpose can be challenging. Purpose will cause you to be misunderstood. But on the other hand, purpose will motivate, inspire, propel, and encourage you. So instead of giving up, giving in, or succumbing to life's misfortunes, you must not lose focus of purpose. You have too much potential, too much possibility to be immobilized. For every bad breakup, every person who betrayed you, God will allow these things in our lives to position us for purpose. You would not be prepared and developed for purpose had God not used these things to position you.

No matter my background, who my parents were, whether I grew up in the suburbs or in the country. No matter how many successful failures I've had, I am here because of purpose. You are purpose; you are not an accident.

Purpose requires preparation. Not only does purpose require preparation, but purpose also requires positioning. When your existence and God's purpose collide, you are unstoppable.

Another one of my favorite passages in scripture comes from Ecclesiastes 3:1–2: "to everything there is a season, and a time to every purpose under the heaven: A time to be born, and a time to die; a time to plant, and a time to pluck up that which is planted…"

We are not born fully grown. We are born infants. We must learn, grow, and develop. We go through stages, and as we grow into ourselves, we cultivate values, interests, aspirations, and goals.

Growth is important; however, too much growth over a short period of time can be dangerous. For example, acromegaly is a rare condition where the body produces too much growth hormone, causing body tissues and bones to grow more quickly. Over time, this leads to abnormally large hands and feet and a wide range of other symptoms.

To get us in position for our purpose as God has designed for our lives, we must fully understand that even though we are dealing with life's problems and all of life's trials, we still have purpose.

Know this, instead of asking, "Why is this happening to me? Why am I going through this?" ask, "What am I supposed to learn from this? What is God trying to show me in this?"

Purpose is not to be selfish. It is not to be arrogant; it is not to be greedy or self-promotional, and it is not to use or abuse. You don't have to cheat, lie, stab anyone in the back, or try to make someone else look bad. We don't have to be jealous of anyone else's gift or talent or take advantage of anyone because our purpose is already set. I don't have to misuse anyone because my purpose is already designed and cannot be altered. Purpose has my name on it, purpose is tailor made for me; therefore, resentment is not necessary; therefore, competition is not necessary. We use what's in our hands—those talents, those abilities, our creativity—and keep forging ahead and positioning ourselves for purpose. Yes, get in position, and purpose will come to fruition.

How do we position ourselves for purpose? We serve our way to purpose. We discover our purpose through serving. Don't take for granted the areas of your influence. It is through serving… our purpose is discovered.

Serving provides growth and positions us to discover our purpose. It is through serving that we can experience different areas to help us discover our purpose. Sometimes that initial area of service leads us to purpose.

Let's look at the story of David. After he was anointed by Samuel to be king in I Samuel 16:11–13, before his purpose manifested, he learned how to be a good steward, commitment, and responsibility. In this season, David learned about the influence in his life as he cared for sheep. If you want to fulfill your purpose, find an area to serve. Serving positions and prepares us to discover purpose.

Look for ways to be a blessing. Live your life, not only focused on you and your dreams and the dreams of your family but live to serve someone else's dream. Take a break from your dreams, your problems, your family, me and mine, and go out of your way for someone else's dream. When you serve others, that is a seed you sow. I heard someone say once, "What you make happen for others, God will make happen for you." When you are good to others, God will make others be good to you. When you are a blessing to others, God will cause others to bless you. When you make it your business to serve others, God will make things happen for you.

God knows how to make things happen for you.

On the way to purpose (the big thing), God will test you in the small things. It may not be the *big thing*, but it is positioning you for purpose. You cannot skip steps and reach your purpose. The way to purpose is not an elevator or escalator. It is a set of steps, and sometimes it is a long staircase where God leads us step by step. Can you serve even though it seems small or insignificant? This is what David did. He was anointed to be the next king of Israel at seventeen years old. The prophet Samuel came to David's father's house unannounced and chose him over seven older brothers.

David did not go to the palace immediately after he was anointed. He went back to the field taking care of the sheep. One day his father asked him to take some lunch to his brothers who were in another city at war. David could have told his father, "I am not an errand boy—my brothers should be serving me. I am next in line to be king." David could have been too proud to do a small thing. Instead, he headed out as his father had wished. When he arrived at their camp, he heard Goliath the champion of the Philistine Army taunting the Israeli army. If David had not been willing to serve in a small, insignificant area, he would have never met his Goliath (purpose). His purpose was hidden in what was small and insignificant. You must be willing to do something small before God can trust you with something big. David was led into his destiny by doing a small, insignificant thing.

You would think when God anointed David to be king, the next step would have been to meet with the commander of the army and strategize with the military. I wonder if your next level is in serving. Would you think it is small and insignificant? Do not put off the opportunity to serve someone. You may have something bigger in your heart, but trust God in the small things. David could have said, "I am a king, not a delivery boy." Your purpose could be waiting for you in your next act of small, insignificant service. This could be your Goliath moment.

David talked with some people in the army and found that there was a huge reward for defeating Goliath. Whoever killed Goliath would get one of the king's daughters as their wife, and their family would be free from paying taxes. When you marry the king's daughter, that means your status will change. With one defeat, David became royalty and found purpose.

The king sent for David. He went to deliver a lunch, and now he was standing in the presence of a king. It is amazing what can happen when you serve. Just for being faithful, just by doing something that seems small or insignificant. You do not know when you will be called on. When it is your time, God will cause you to be in the right place at the right time. He will cause you to be seen. He will mention your name. Don't stumble over the rock looking for a mountain.

David went out with a slingshot and five stones, defeated Goliath, and his status changed. Just by serving. God will suddenly thrust you to a new level. God knows how to position you for purpose. You may not see this happening. David did not. He was just delivering a lunch. He was serving in what seemed like a small, insignificant area. God will make things happen that you never dreamed would happen, all because you were willing to serve.

David did not deliver the lunch with an agenda thinking he would meet the king. He was just serving. He was not trying to push his way or manipulate a situation. He was just doing what his father asked him to do, and the opportunity came to him. When you serve with the right attitude, you do not have to convince anyone to make way for you or grant you favor. God will make way and give you favor. The blessing will come to you.

If you just keep serving…
Serving when no one is looking.
Serving when no one says thank you.
Serving when you feel like it and when you do not.
Serving like your life depends on it.
God will open doors you never imagined or dreamed.
God will thrust you into purpose.

When you serve not expecting anything in return, serve from your heart with the right attitude, always considering others more than yourself, using the gifts and talents that have been trusted to your hands. Use those gifts and talents to bless others who can't pay you back, not for your own gratification. Serve with humility, obedience, passion, thoughtfulness and without hesitation. Those you serve will speak well of you and honor your service.

When you do everything to make someone successful, you automatically shine. When you help build someone else's dream—sow into someone else's dream—God lifts you up. When those you serve are lifted, you will be lifted, and your purpose becomes clearer. You walk from the infancy of your purpose into the realization of it, and things come full circle as noted in Romans 8:28, "And we know that all things work together for good to those who love God, to those who are called according to His purpose."

God sees your works of service as they assist in helping others.

The power of serving changes things around you and inspires others to position themselves for purpose. Do not discount the power of serving, as it speaks volumes. The ripple effect is perpetual and sets the stage for your purpose. As with David, his small act of service led him to be king over a nation.

Continue to serve because your moment is coming. Your Goliath moment is just around the corner. Don't give up, don't give in, and don't fall short. God is not a man that He should lie (Numbers 23:19) therefore, hold on to His promises, and lean not toward your own understanding

(Proverbs 3:5: Trust in the LORD with all thine heart; and lean not unto thine own understanding), and serve.

Isn't it amazing that by serving others, God positions you for purpose? He wants you to be successful. He wants you to be fulfilled, and it starts with serving others. With each act of service, a new level is set, a new door is open, more of your purpose is revealed. With each act of service, new hope is released, new connections are made, deeper character is revealed, potential is unleashed, and more of God's grace is afforded. With each act of service, your faith grows stronger, you motivate and inspire others. You increase the faith of those you serve, and you strengthen their relationship with God through serving, and courage is built in you. With each act of service, you compel others to pass it on, causing an epidemic of kindness to be released, causing a legacy in your generation and those to come of Purpose Achievers.

If you are not sure where to start your journey of service, start small—do something you love to do. Do something you are passionate about with your family, friends, neighbors, church, job, strangers, or anonymous acts of kindness. Not only will this plant seeds for your purpose, but it will also cause you to think outside of yourself. Acts of service also help you to pull someone else out of their pasture and position them for purpose. If someone is hungry and you provide a meal, it gives them the strength to continue moving forward and not give up. If someone needs shelter, and you provide a room, it gives them warmth and restores their confidence in humanity. If someone is angry, and you lend an ear and provide some solace, it could save a life—or maybe two. If someone doesn't have family and you act as a surrogate, this act could potentially stave off suicide due to loneliness. A simple smile or hello may be all that someone needs to make it through the day. A word of encouragement may help someone find the strength to continue to fight off a debilitating disease. You may never know what is going through someone's mind or what someone may be dealing with, and your act of service and kindness may be the one thing they need to get to their next level. Know that your act of service is the angel in someone's life, their saving grace—God showing up in the shape of you.

Service is not just doing an act, but it is also performing that act with grace and humility. This could be that small, insignificant thing that could position and push you into purpose. No matter how big of an impact you have in this world, it doesn't really count unless it is in service to another.

Now that you are informed on what to expect regarding your purpose, you can see how clearly the trials of life that ultimately push and position us for our purpose, are not to serve you but others. Your purpose grows with your service to others. Their purpose grows with your service to others, and that purpose creates a legacy of purpose for generations to come. The more you serve, the more your purpose grows. The more you serve, the more you are elevated. The more you serve, the more you grow in God. The more you grow in God, the better your service becomes to others. As your service grows you in God, your character is more like God, your walk is more like God, your talk is more like God, your thoughts are more like God. You are more like God—humble, thankful, grateful, and willing. You now serve without a second thought. It is second nature for you. You seek out those who are in need. You are always thinking about what you can do to help others. There is no more "self-thought," but "what can I do to make someone else's load easier?" "How can I make someone else's life better?" You're always thinking of how you can make things better for others. You go the extra mile to show you care, and you are a faithful. You inspire, you are motivated to challenge others to position themselves for purpose.

Whether you are a believer or secular, you must know that everything in life, including the trials and tribulations, are designed to enable us to reach a goal called purpose. Think of trials and tribulations as training that will position you for a goal of purpose. Our trials and tribulations come with a reward—purpose—and our greatest misery becomes our greatest ministry. Purpose is not just on you; purpose is in you. Get in position, and you will become directly in line with the thing you were designed for.

Before you know it, without any effort, you will be walking, talking, and living in purpose, and because of this, your life will be a blessing—not only to yourself but to those around you. The blessing will begin to trickle down and become a domino effect, and with that legacy of purpose, you will begin a cycle of generational purpose.

I will end this chapter with a scripture that I build my life around, Proverbs 19:21: Many are the plans in a man's (woman's) heart, but it is the Lord's purpose that prevails.

You can plan out your life, who you will marry, how many children you will have, where you will go to school, where you will retire. You can choose all of these, but you cannot choose how God positions us for purpose.

Joice M. Sawyer

Joice M. Sawyer is a native of Newark, New Jersey, and a product of the East Orange New Jersey Public School System. After graduating from high school, she continued her education at Virginia Commonwealth University in Richmond, Virginia, where she studied rehabilitative counseling. In 2002, she received a certificate in biblical studies from Calvary Bible Institute. In June 2003, she received a bachelor of ministry degree in Christian counseling, and in June 2005, she satisfied the course requirements for a master of theological studies degree from National Bible Seminary.

Since 1997, she has served faithfully in ministry as an associate minister of Greater Mount Calvary Holy Church in Washington, DC, under the tutelage and leadership of Pastors Alfred and Susie Owens.

Joice is an ordained elder in the Mount Calvary Holy Churches, Inc. She previously served as adjunct professor at National Bible College and Seminary and currently serves as adjunct professor at Calvary Bible Institute, assistant instructor at Calvary Bible Institute, director of the Adjutants Academy of the Mount Calvary Holy Churches, and has previously served as team leader and secretary on the Evangelistic Board, member of the budget committee; and assistant Sunday school teacher of the Greater Mount Calvary Holy Church in Washington, DC. She currently hosts The Servant's Call on Facebook Live and YouTube where she pours into servants of the Kingdom of God. She enjoys Broadway plays and spending time with family and friends.

Joice is married to Pastor John D. Sawyer and serves alongside him at Mt. Calvary Missionary Baptist Church, Temple Hills, Maryland.

Purpose is a Journey to be Lived

EZREAONNE JACKSON

It has been an incredible journey to purpose. After seven decades of life, I have discovered through reflective thought and experience and surmised through assessment of the numerous individuals I have had the privilege to counsel, mentor, and pastor that purpose is a journey. In this quick-fix, microwave culture, we have somehow deceived ourselves into thinking that purpose happens overnight.

Just think for a moment how exciting a planned vacation, a trip with the family for a memorable holiday to a sagged parent's or grandparent's home, or even going on a special date. The feeling of exhilaration motivates your whole being and catapults you to the journey of preparation. The thought of the destination is the antecedent, and the hope of the destination is the operant that moves us to action. There would be no motion or moving forward if there were not a purpose.

As we see into the core of who we are and our relationship with the

God of Abraham, Isaac, and Jacob mentioned in the Holy Bible and taught to many of us in Sunday school, we can relate to the possibility of the greatness of God in our life. I am convinced that everyone needs to discover the core of their existence as it is the wellspring from which they start the journey of mindful awareness and the comprehending in order to gather the significance of the lessons learned from the past.

With that knowledge, we are encouraged to embrace the future. God has always been the core of existence for me, although it has taken me years in my journey to fully understand that He is the same God of Abraham, Isaac, Jacob, and Ezreaonne. Without a core, it is not easy to have an intentional value system that is needed to orbit who a person is. The values of the heart determine an individual's future and are syncopated in harmony with the behavior produced by it. This system of balance enables an individual to stay the course.

We must somehow come to terms with the creator to understand his purpose for us. No amount of substance abuse, sexual promiscuity, or financial or intellectual prowess can alleviate our necessity of connecting, even if that connection rejects Him. At the least individuals will know their core and its values, whether they are godly or ungodly. It is all about the journey to the destination. Proverbs 14:12 (KJV), "There is a way which seemeth right unto a man, but the end thereof are the ways of death."

This author hopes that the readers will discover the lessons learned through the plethora of valleys, alleys, caves, roads, highways, and freeways experienced in their life that will take them to the place of the new places that will enhance their full journey. Breathe and invest in moments of mindfulness as you read through this chapter. May you find solace and understand you do not have to rush through life. Take one day at a time.

While safe as an embryo, we are unconscious of the journey that will lead us through the birthing canal to awaken in a world designed to begin our life journey, which is not cognitively realized. We may or may not have parents or guardians who intentionally shaped our lives to produce character and integrity with a sense of directional purpose. We consciously followed with probably some lack of apprehension and ambiguity to their instructions as we submitted to the enculturation of our faith community, school systems, and the communal cultural traditions of our family and community.

I recall watching with amazement when the United States opened its gates to the refugees from the Vietnam War and their ability to integrate into our society as entrepreneurs. I had not experienced witnessing a young child at the cash register managing a financial transaction. I had wondered why I had not seen little Afro-American children or even myself trained to be confident at such an early stage in life. We all have windows in time when something impresses us so profoundly that it will resurface to help us understand the nature of our journey. As a result of my journey in life and this profound window experience, I am presently working with children as a behavior therapist in mental health. The shaping and chaining of life events (mother, grandmother, civil rights and women's rights advocate, pastor, teacher, and family human service provider) is the evidence of that one instance in observing with awe a little Vietnamese child work a cash register, which influenced my life.

What is so fascinating is that we are constantly navigating on metaphoric streets called Journey Avenue, Expressway to Tomorrow, and Business Route Right Away. We are inundated with the to-do list. According to psychologist Abram Maslow and his hierarchy of needs, belonging is essential to our existence. As a community, it is crucial to develop a mindset that everyone in the community plays a significant role that either positively influences or detours a person's goal or purpose. Assessing the value of what each person brings to life is a tool needed to make the right choice that synchronizes with our purpose intelligently. One of the most powerful influencers in my life today is Dr. Dennis Myles Golphin, a Christian scholar and biblicist. In the 2022 Bravo Conference held in Goldsboro, North Carolina, during a panel discussion, Dr. Golphin brought to light the concept of three-three-three concerning purpose. He stated that Jesus spent thirty years preparing for purpose, three-and-a-half years doing ministry, and three hours dying to accomplish his goal.

As a clergywoman, I have endeavored to be hermeneutically sound in teaching and living the mandates of the principles of the Gospel. Because the Christian faith community has a broad scope of denominations, church edicts, doctrines, and traditions, it has become a complex and paradoxical society. Hermeneutics is a science of interpreting scriptures from the objective and not a subjective standard. John 18:37 (KJV), "Pilate, therefore, said unto him, 'Art thou a king then?' Jesus answered, 'Thou sayest that I am a king. To this end was I born, and for this cause came I into the world, that I should bear witness unto the truth. Every one that is of the truth heareth my voice.'"

The manuscript quotes Jesus as saying why he was born. From extrapolating the various scriptures of his disciples and other writers who expressed his purpose, such as John in 1 John 3:8, it is a common thread of belief that Jesus' purpose was to destroy the works of the devil by paying the cost for the sin issue that happens in the garden. He came to bear witness to the Father and Creator's plan and implement it. In doing so, He lived on this earth for thirty-three-and-a-half years, thirty years of preparation, started serving in the capacity of ministry for three-and-a-half years, and died on the cross for hours.

The Preparation

Luke 3:52 (KJV), "And Jesus increased in wisdom and stature, and in favor with God and men."

We should have a cognitive view of the enculturation (home, school, religious institutions, and cultural norms) that have molded our concepts and constructs. Those constructs are the lens from which we see life and are the motivational voices that determine our choices. Those choices are critical and create a trajectory that impacts our future endeavors.

While pensive in thought and the perusal of the myriad of individuals who have inspired our community and my life, the most recent revealing of the first National Basketball Association Black female chief executive officer Cynt Marshall who was brought to attention in our Activating Kingdom Initiative membership thread via video by Waynette Duty who is a prolific personality and ardent about communicating relevant information to the faith community.

Cynt Marshall was prepared for her role as she successfully navigated through discrimination, cancer, and toxic culture. She shares in an interview about her beginnings in the housing projects in Richmond, California, her abusive father who broke her nose when she was fifteen trying to help her mother from his abusive attack, and the impact of her parents' separation played in her life. Marshall was the first black cheerleader at the University of California, Berkeley, during the latter part of the 1970s. Amazed at how she spent forty years with AT&T climbing the corporate ladder and how all the setbacks and setups prepared her for who she is today at the helm of the Dallas Mavericks, Marshall shares that the core of her existence is her faith, modeled and taught by her mother who took her to church. She does not deny that all other values and interests orbit around her faith principles (Scipioni, 2021).

If we allow ourselves the time to be in the moment of successful people carefully and note the specifics of their life's journey, we will be able to see the delicate thread that is common to each of them—the heartache, the disappointments, the trauma, and the grit to get through it all! There is a light at the end of the proverbial tunnel; we must survive the darkness. The dark places are our teachers, and the lessons are learned because other senses are sharpened in the absence of the lack of our comfort zone crutches.

Of course, Jesus had an advantage because He knew He was God's son but let us consider that He allowed His divinity to yield while He maneuvered through life in His humanity. The paradox of God standing in an obscured place and His ability to fully experience humanity will remain a mystery to be fully revealed to us in the future. His preparation years were accepted as He developed naturally within His community. As an infant, He was born in a manger, relocated as He and His family escaped to Egypt, returned home, was taught His father's skills, and lived under Jewish law. All of this is to leave a legacy and example for us.

We do not know much about Jesus's thirty years of maturation, but we understand the cycle of life and how each moment shapes who we are to become.

You have been purposed for what is to come and have been called to do. It does not matter when you physically heard the call or sensed an inner nudging or not; the call shaped your life as you were built to thrive through the preparation years. Take a moment and assess where you may be at this moment in your life.

I have had the opportunity to study each ten-year interval of my seventy decades and realized that an orchestrated pattern of incidences prepared me for these challenging times, specially designed for my purposed assignment. Those days of preparation left an indelible cognitive message and lesson that sustained me with grit to push through each turmoil, tragedy, disappointment, and traumatic moment. Each moment was impacted with survival tools ascertained from the previous moment.

The Ministry

Internship

Matthew 23:11 (KJV), "But he that is greatest among you shall be your servant."

I heard a snippet from a podcast, which included a comment from Oprah Winfrey stating, "Legacy is the influence you leave anyone's life you have crossed." Serving depicts the lesson of preparation and is our crossing over to full maturation when we genuinely enjoy what we are doing. The dynamics of mastering our idiosyncrasies is a mighty feat. Carl Jung (1876–1961) was a Swiss psychiatrist and psychoanalyst who introduced analytical psychology (Fordham, 2022). His work concerning the subconscious of man and its shadow was intriguing as the truth of our mandate to carry the truth of the Gospel, which reveals the nature of man who must be reckoned with (https://youtu.be/OhzBo0dZNpY). If we pretend or deny that we have no shadow (jealousy, strife, anger, hatred, lust), we impede our growth and cannot have a healthy relationship with ourselves or others. We can refer to the Bible's analogy given to us by Jesus in Matthew 7:5 as He expounded that we must take the beam out of our eye before we take a stick out of someone else's (paraphrased by me).

Dr. Dharius Daniels, in his book *Relational Intelligence*, gives us insight into the significance of evaluating relationships and assessing what kind of behavioral response should be relegated to those individuals we encounter. John 2:24 (KJV), "But Jesus did not commit himself unto them, because He knew all men." Assessing the people who encircle our life is a learned behavior. It is a behavior that is essential to our growth and our influential prowess as entrepreneurs and leaders. Assessing your community is a core factor as we navigate from preparation to serving because the two entities finely morph into each other, causing discrimination too difficult to differentiate.

The preparation prepares us for what we are purposed to do. All purposes are centered around assisting our neighbor in some way or another. Our passions draw us to our purpose. Those passions may or may not have been conscientious as the core of its function but only realized by an individual who reaches a plateau of self-realization and clarity of purpose. As much as some individuals work to get away from the God factor, it becomes impossible to escape because of the finite of man and the infinity of the Creator.

We can validate that all we do is predominately centered around what and how we facilitate each other. Whether we choose to be a farmer, mental health provider, politician, physician, mortician, pilot, an educator, clergy, an entertainer, et cetera, they all enable and assist a commodity or product that facilitates an end use for humanity. There is no getting away from the simple word of *serving*.

How well individuals serve depends upon their motivation. There is a science used in applied behavior analysis called "motivational operant." Knowing what motivates a client to respond to the teaching of an appropriate behavior, the therapist must understand what motivates the client. The therapist uses the knowledge of the client's motivation as an operant to assist in creating appropriate behaviors repetitiously and rewards them for doing so until the client has instilled that behavior in their psychological repertoire. While a person serves, it's vital that an honest self-assessment of why they serve be considered. The impetus defines the inner character and the ways and means (integrity) by which they will reach their goals.

Jesus' motivation was to do the will of His Father. His will and His Father's will were so entangled, like that of the bone and the marrow, as separating the bone and marrow in the early century was impossible as medical procedures were not as advanced as they are today.

Individuals who are solely motivated by money, power, and status will reap the benefits and consequences of that operant. Our society has witnessed the downfall of powerful men and women who have accomplished many successful ventures and acquired astronomical amounts of financial wealth. Looking closely at the emptiness of their lives, we are in awe of how none of their accomplishments brought them happiness or peace of mind. The vacuum of power, money, and status is ego driven and not heart centered. The treasure of the heart reveals the character of the soul.

In his famous speech "I Have a Dream," Reverend Martin Luther King, Jr., resonates with me as I was born in Jackson, Mississippi, in 1951. Reverend King states, "I have a dream that one day even the state of Mississippi, a state sweltering with the heat of oppression, will be transformed into an oasis of freedom and justice (US Embassy, 2017). Although my parents were part of the 1960 migration as Black folks from the south escaping the Jim Crow atrocities to find a better quality of life on the North and West coasts, those horrors did not escape my DNA.

I suggest the reader take a moment and write down what preparation and serving have taught them about their journey. What can be extrapolated from its experiences? There is a deep well of brilliance and wealth in an individual mind with tools of insight, honesty, objectivity, and cognition. Survival leads to thriving, and thriving leads to the ability to trail blaze for someone unaware of the pitfalls and emotional climate needed while reaching the finality of purpose.

The Purpose

It is finished!

John 9:30 (KJV), "When Jesus, therefore, had received the vinegar, He said, it is finished: and He bowed his head, and gave up the ghost."

Rustling and wrestling through preparation courses and defining the reasons and clarity of purpose are maturation plateaus. While one's past is not the definition of who they presently are, it is the meticulous tools that help shape who they have become or are becoming. The journey should be filled with the compilation of the tears of joy and grief, the experience of the lost and found, the aftermath of expectation and disappointment, the emotions of fear and courage, the gift of love and the damage of hate, the knowledge of failure and success, birth and death while facing light and darkness with brevity and confidence.

"It is finished" were the second-to-last words of Jesus on the cross, accomplishing His purpose of redeeming man from His fallen nature and the consequences of death that preceded it. According to Biblical history, it took Jesus only a few hours to fulfill His ultimate purpose. Though His last hours were agonizing beyond human comprehension, he did not leave a model for us to finish in the same fashion as He did. He left us with the concept of completing the purpose.

Conclusion

When an individual reaches the maturation of their purpose, the motivating factor is to leave a legacy to the next generation. When individuals think that legacy is a financial empire or inheritance, focus can be lost on what matters. We cannot negate that need for economic propriety as lucrative necessities to build enterprises and sustain the livelihoods of stakeholders and their families. The legacy we must leave is the journey of purpose and the finale of passing the proverbial torch or baton. We have seen it displayed by poet-artists like Maya Angelou, civil rights activist and clergyman Reverend Martin Luther King, Jr., actors like Denzel Washington and Viola Davis, and political leaders such as Barack Obama and Vice President Kamala Harris. We all play a part in leaving a legacy to our children, immediate family, and community.

Your journey to purpose is a phenomenon that should be regarded as your most important asset. It should be carefully guarded and passed to others with thought and agility. The purpose will be your legacy, which leaves imprints that will impact on others along their journey paths. The journey was yesterday; it is now and tomorrow. Your last breath on this earth and transition from this life to eternal does not stop. Someone will carry the torch you have left to illuminate the path to success of those you have empowered. Travel well, my friend.

Ezreaonne Jackson

Ezreaonne Jackson was born in Jackson, Mississippi, on January 14, 1951, to the late Warren L. Jackson and Yvonne Edwards. Her life's faith dynamics were Baptist (her father's preference) and African Methodist Episcopalian (her mother's preference). Her maternal grandfather, late Right Reverend Dr. Watson Edwards, was an elder of the African Methodist Episcopal faith and founded Edwards Chapel in Coldwater, Mississippi. After experiencing a personal encounter with Jesus at the age of nineteen, she accepted Christ as her savior.

She has a twenty-year career tenure in the business arena using her administrative skills and human resources and sales. Her employment portfolio includes Kaiser Steel, AT&T, Dean Forwarding and Kelly Services, and Snelling Personnel. She is licensed with the Board of Mental Health Counseling as a Qualified Mental Health Professional actively involved in the mental health field as a behavior therapist. Her LLC is a mentorship program. She continues to be overseer of several church leaders as a ministry coach and gospel speaker and preacher.

She received her bachelor of arts religious studies degree in biblical studies from the Regency Christian College in Jacksonville, Florida; received an honorary doctorate in ministry from Trinity Bible College in Richmond, Virginia: and is an alumni of the Graduate School of Episcopal Studies. She has received her bachelor of science degree in human services with a concentration in family and youth services at the University of Phoenix.

She is a devoted mother, beloved godmother, and a grandmother to six beautiful children.

Love on Purpose

ROZ BROWN

> "Beloved let us love one another, for love is God
> and every one who loves is born of God… God is love!"
> —1 John 4:7, 16

For the next few moments, I want to talk about love.

The power of intentional love.

Love on purpose.

I'll never forget growing up in a Christian home. As children, the first scripture my siblings and I learned was John 3:16, "For God so loved the world that He gave His only begotten Son, that whosoever believeth on Him should not perish but have everlasting life…"

The second scripture we learned was from 1 John 4:16, "God is love." It was imperative that we learned the ultimate message of love. The harsh reality is there is enough hatred, fear, and darkness in the world. Therefore, we must be the love, we must be the light, and the world will know we are Christians by our love.

The love God gave to us, through the gift of His son, Jesus, was not an accident; nor was it coincidence. It was not as ordinary love. It was extraordinary love. It was intentional. It was an entire love agenda. God loved us so much on purpose. God loved us so much that He gave His only son, Jesus, to die on a cross on purpose. God forgave all of our sins on purpose.

Let's give them something to talk about. Let's talk about love.

Love Facts

1. God is love.
2. Love is God.
3. Love is God's other name.
4. Love is who God is.
5. Love is what God does.

When you understand this, it becomes literally impossible to "look for love in all the wrong places."

Because God is love, God's most prevalent characteristics are also characteristics of love.

God Is, So Love Is...

1. Omniscient—all knowing. God knows everything. Therefore, love knows everything.
2. Omnipotent—all powerful. God can do anything. Therefore, love can do anything.
3. Omnipresent—all present. God is everywhere. Therefore, love is everywhere.

On your best day, love is there. In the darkest night of your soul, love is still there.

Life is a journey, but love will lead you every step of the way.

To love is to literally see the face of God. To love is literally to hear the voice of God. To love is to literally feel the breath of God. To love is to literally know the peace of God.

In every moment or encounter of life, we either teach love, or we teach fear. Pick one, beloved.

Love in your mind produces love in your life. This is heaven.

Fear in your mind produces fear in your life. This is hell.

In life we are either teaching love, or we are teaching fear.

What are you teaching? What are you producing?

We Were Born to Love

When a baby is born, he has a natural instinct for love and affection—a gentle touch, the sound of a lullaby or a warm hug can instantly calm fears, tears, discomfort, and traumas. For example, often a crying child will instantly become silent and comforted at the sight of a mother because the child knows love has come to the rescue. When Jesus gave His life for our sins, that was love to the rescue.

Jesus Said, "Just Love Them"

Jesus taught the message of love to everyone He met. Jesus was on a love mission everywhere He went. The book of John 21:17 (NLT) says, "A third time Jesus asked 'Simon, son of John, do you love me?' He said, 'Lord, you know I love you.' Jesus said, 'Then feed my sheep.'" I believe Jesus was teaching us to understand that love is as love does and love comes with obligation to take care of one another, cover one another, to protect one another, to support one another, and to strengthen one another.

In 1 Peter 4:8 (NLT), Peter says "Love each other deeply, because love covers a multitude of sins." We say we love, but how often does our love cover one another's messes, mistakes, bad decisions, poor choices, faults, failures, and bottom-line sins? We are quick to point fingers, but where is the love? We are quick to spread rumors, but where is the love? I believe the day we are living in is a prime case for love. Let's find and feed lost sheep. Let's show the love.

Love is Not Always Easy, but it is Necessary

There are times in life when love is complicated—when love's answers are hard to find, when love makes questionable decisions, when love seems to be so far away—but real love will always find a way. Love will show up to care, to share, to be there or be square. Yes, love will find a way.

Love Does the Right Thing, Because It's the Right Thing to Do

On another occasion in the book of 1 John 14:15 (NLT), Jesus says, "If you love me keep my commandments… He who has my commandments and keeps them, it is he who loves me." I believe when Jesus spoke of commandments, He was speaking of the things He was teaching about life and love. He was teaching that love not only hears, but love obeys. And our daily prayer should be *Lord, please give me a do right mind. Help me to live right, teach me to do right, I just want to be right.* There are times when we will have to fight the feelings and the tug-of-war between right and wrong, but even when it's hard, love does what's right because it's the right thing to do. And love wins every time.

What's Love Got to Do with It?

I was in my senior year of high school in 1984 when The Tina Turner released the song that asked the infamous question "What's love got to do with it?" She went on to say who needs a heart when a heart can be broken.

Perhaps she was oblivious to the fact that God is love and love is God, and if this is true, then love has everything to do with it. The reality is the failure is not in love. The failure is in us. Yes, life will bring disappointments. Yes, relationships will break hearts, bring tears and pain, but the real truth is love never fails. Yes, there are times hearts will even be broken, but Psalm 147:3 (NLT) says, "He mends the broken hearted and binds up their wounds." So then the question to Tina Turner may be, Was it really love? Because real love has everything to do with it.

Let's Be Serial Lovers

We are children of God, and as children of God, we should have the nature of God, and the nature of God is love. But sadly we live in a day and time where books, movies, media, and news sensationalize the darkness and evilness of serial killers. People will pay to sit and watch hours of the horror and torture of the life of a sick-minded serial killer, which will only feed demonic strongholds of the spirits.

But it's time we rise up and dispel this day and hour of darkness. God is looking for, birthing, and raising up serial lovers—those who will love without hesitation and without reservation; those who will love again and again. Wherever there's a void, love will fill it. We live love, we give love, we shed love, we spread love. It's love for the win.

What the World Needs Now Is Love Sweet Love

This is more than just a song, it's a mission. Love should be our ultimate life mission.

People may not be like you, people may not believe like you, but love is always in order. The Bible teaches unconditional love; however, unconditional love is not condoning love. I don't have to condone all you do to love you without conditions. I may not agree with your actions or choices, but I love you unconditionally, and my love for you will not change.

What Is Love?

"Love is patient and kind. Love is not jealous or boastful or proud or rude. It does not demand its own way. It is not irritable, and it keeps no record of being wronged. It does not rejoice about injustice but rejoices whenever the truth wins out. Love never gives up, never loses faith, is always hopeful, and endures through every circumstance" (1 Corinthians 13:4–7, NLT).

This is what the Bible teaches about love and the way we should love. No, it's not always easy, but when this is our guide and focus, our love walk is clearer.

It's Giving Love

Love isn't put in our hearts to stay and love isn't love till you give it away, someone once said.

Thoughts of love are kind, but they don't really serve anyone. Tell someone you love them. Tell them Jesus loves them. Show them you love them. Show them Jesus loves them. Little things show love—stopping by to visit someone you haven't seen in a while; a phone call just to say hello, I love you or hear someone's voice; a bouquet of flowers; having lunch with a child at school; going with a friend to church; going to support someone at a game; a walk on the beach; a cup of coffee; a cup of tea; a picnic in the park; a candle in the dark. It's the little things that mean so much, it's the little things that show the love.

Love Is a Verb—An Action Word—and Actions Speak Louder Than Words

It's nice to talk about love, but it's so much better to be about love.

Love doesn't always speak; sometimes love just listens, sometimes love is just mere presence. However, there must be an action—and sometimes even inaction or a reaction—but ultimately there is a demonstration in the true expression of love.

Song of Solomon is a collaboration of love stories/poems in the form of songs addressed for the most part by a man to a woman, but some are by a woman to a man. These songs have been interpreted by Jews as a picture of the relationship between God and his people and by Christians as a picture of the relationship of Christ to the church.

Song 8:7 (NLT) reads, "Many waters cannot quench love."

This is so powerful because life happens, but love is everlasting. We saw this in the Florida hurricanes as homes, lives, boats, and massive properties were swept away. Love can never be extinguished. Love will always burn, no matter what. It's been said that if love ever was then love always is.

Song 8:6 (NLT) says, "Love is stronger than death and more powerful than the grave."

Love raises the bar. Have you ever noticed when someone is in love, they always want to do things to show it—go out on dates, buy flowers, play love songs, talk for hours, and the list goes on. It's because love raises the bar, and there is a desire to reach higher.

I Don't Fall in Love, I Rise in Love

Many years ago, I decided to never "fall in love" again. Why, you ask? Because falling hurts, period. Love should always take you higher. From better to better, from richer to richer, from greater to greater, from Glory to Glory, from strength to strength. Rise in love, strive in love, thrive in love, and above all, let love live big in you every day.

Love Is a Lifestyle

Loving is how I'm living. My day doesn't determine my love. My love determines my day. I live to love big every day.

When I got married in 1986 at a very young age to an also young, talented musician/college student Zeke Williams, we were married in a beautiful sanctuary in Richmond, Virginia, by my father, Bishop James Ferguson Brown Jr. and Bishop J Delano Ellis, Bishop Ellis charged us as a couple to try to beat each other loving each other every day. He said let our only competition be to see who could love the other the most. And even though we were only married a few short years, those words still challenge me today. Try your best to out love each other on purpose every day. Perhaps that may be why after the storm of divorce subsided, a new relationship of love and respect arose and remains to this very day.

We must live a life of love on purpose every day.

We should be on a daily assignment to out love each other.

It is so important that love be our guide. We should let the light of love guide us, Psalm 112:4 (NLT) says, "When darkness overtakes the righteous, the light will come bursting in."

Love Is Who We Are

They will know we are Christians by our love.

The love we show one to another should identify us. When the world sees us, they should see Jesus. When they work with us, they should work with Jesus. When they live near us, they should live near Jesus. Jesus said in Matthew 25:40, when you love/help them, you love me.

Love Principles

1. Practice love on purpose every day. Practice makes perfect.
2. Study to show yourself approved (2 Timothy 2:15).
3. Ponder love on purpose every day. Whatsoever things are good whatsoever things are lovely, whatsoever thing are of a good report think on these things (Philippians 4:8).
4. Pursue love on purpose every day. Go hard after it—go hard or go home.
5. The Kingdom suffers violence, but the violent takes it by force (Mathew 11:12).
6. Pen love on purpose every day. Journal it, just write it. You can begin by saying, I know God loves me because…

> "Write the vision and make it plain…"
> —Habakkuk 2:2

7. Prepare for love on purpose every day. If you stay ready, you won't have to get ready. Keep watch for you know not the day or hour (Matthew 25:1–13).

We Shed Love

We were born of love, for love, by love, and to love.

The love of God is shed abroad in our hearts by the Holy Ghost (Romans 5:5 NLT).

As a young teenage girl with a strange hunger, heart, and passion for preaching and the Word of God, I will never forget hearing my uncle Bishop Ronald E Brown from Orangeburg, South Carolina, preach a message saying Christians should never have to "learn" to love. He said, "I've heard saints say I'm learning to love them." No, we don't learn to love. Love is our nature. We love by nature. We are loved by nature. We are lovers by nature. It's our natural instinct. He said cats and dogs don't learn to shed hair, dogs don't learn to bark, snakes don't learn to shed skin, trees don't learn to shed leaves, and saints/Christians don't learn to love. We were born to love. We have the nature of God, which is love. God is love, and children of God are children of love.

Love is our light. We shine and show love by doing good deeds. Everywhere we go, we let love shine through us.

Love is fruit. Fruit has seeds, and seeds are for reproduction; therefore, our love should always be producing more.

Who can love your children the most?

My grandson Noah likes to say he's my favorite. Sometimes in the morning when I head out for work, he'll say, "I love you, Yaya Roz." I'll say, "I love you more, Noah." He'll say, "I love you more, more." I'll say, "I love you more, more, more." Finally, he'll say, "Man, this could go on forever."

Love In, Fear Out

"There is no fear in love, but perfect love casteth out all fear: because fear hath torment. He that feareth is not made perfect in love" (1 John 4:18, KJV).

Love is one of the most powerful weapons we possess. Many years ago, when I lived in Virginia Beach and was a part of The New Jerusalem Church of God in Christ, my Bishop Barnett Karl Thoroughgood would often say when preaching, whenever you see "eth," it means continually (i.e., casteth, feareth), and looking at words from that perspective brings in a whole new light. Love has the power to push fear out of our lives and minds, and in to the sea, to rise no more against us. That's love, and that's a powerful thing. One of the most profound basic grammar lessons I learned was from my ninth-grade English teacher at St. Gertrude Catholic High School, Mrs. Mary Oreadon, who consistently emphasized, "Whenever you see the word *but*, you can disregard everything that came before it. *But* perfect love (continually) casteth out all fear.

Do we really understand the life-changing power in love that we possess?

It is so important that we speak and decree love over our lives daily. I am love, I am loved, I give love, I receive love, I'm in love, love is in me.

Love lives perpetually in me, and I live perpetually in love.

My help is in the name of love, and I meditate on it day and night.

Where love abides, fear cannot stay.

Where love lives, fear leaves.

Love comes, fear goes.

Love in, fear out.

Let go and let love.

Let's go love.

My dearly beloved, love and beloved.

We Did It for Love

When asked the question why we do what we do, as children of God, we answer, we do it for love. We did it for love, it's all about love.

Many years ago, back in the eighties, our church, Jerusalem Holy

Church in Richmond, Virginia, recorded a project entitled, *For a Little Bit of Love*. On that album, my mother, Chief Apostle Olive C. Brown, preached the message of love, which she still preaches to this day. She wrote the theme song, which said:

> *Don't you know the world is dying for a little bit of love, everywhere you hear men sighing, for a little bit of love, for the love that's right or wrong fill some hearts with hope and song they have waited Oh so long…*

This world is longing for love; this world is dying for love. I've seen children uprooted and abandoned longing for love, seniors dropped off at care facilities where families never return to love. They are left and forsaken by love, longing for love and so many people dying to be loved.

No Greater Love

I honestly believe one of the greatest songs ever, was written by my brother-in-law David L. Allen of Winston Salem, North Carolina, who wrote a song called "No Greater Love."

> *Jesus went to Calvary, to save a wretch like you and me, that's love, that's love.*

> *They hung Him high; they stretched Him wide, He hung His head, for me He died, that's love, that's love.*

> *But that's not how the story ends three days later He rose again, that's love, that's love.*

> *There is no greater love than a man would lay down His life for a friend. That's love, that's love.*

Every Easter, churches and choirs throughout this nation and the world ring out this gospel melody to this very day because Calvary truly is the greatest love of all.

Love Is Contagious

In 2020, the world experienced what is believed to be the greatest virus spread ever in our lifetime. The spread of the COVID-19/coronavirus, which caused a pandemic that was absolutely unimaginable. A worldwide virus that could not be contained literally shut the entire world down and filled it with the widest spread of sickness, death, and devastation ever seen, all through a small, contagious germ/virus that literally took our breath away and changed the history of our lives forever.

Our love should be so strong. It should be contagious, uncontainable, and unstoppable love. It should change our hearts, our homes, our communities, our world, and our lives forever.

Love Out Loud

As a child growing up, my grandmother, whom we called "GaGa," Bishop Annie Bullock Chamblin had a huge house, which seemed to be the biggest house in the world to my little eyes. In that home was our sweet Mama Dot. Dorothy "Dottie" Jones was at that time my grandmother's live-in housekeeper. That house had so many memories, one of which was the big windows. They seemed to go up to the sky. When I was old enough to reach the cord on the blinds, Gaga and Mama Dot would say, "Go open up the house and let the sunshine in. Don't sit around in a dark house. The sun is shining. Let it in. It's waiting to come in, but you have to let it in." That's how love is. We must let it out, and we must let it in.

The scripture in Psalms 112:4 (TLB) says, "When darkness overtakes him, light will come bursting in. He is kind and merciful—."

Just like the crowds on Black Friday morning, love will come bursting in.

Love Is Light

What is the light? Jesus says, "I am the Light of the world," but when he left this earthly world and went back to His Father in heaven, He said, "You are the light of the world." Yes, we are the light of the world, like a city on a hill that cannot be hidden.

But what is our light? Love is our light.

Every day we were born to shine. Eat love and glitter for breakfast, and shine all day.

It's time to let love shine.

Love should never be hidden. Love should never be a foreign language. Love should be our common thread, especially in our homes, our lives, our churches, and our schools.

Many times, my youngest foster grand will come and say, "I want to come hug you. Huggies, please. Can I come hug you?"

That's her way of getting away to me and letting her love shine on me.

He Loves Me, He Loves Me More

I can also remember growing up in Richmond, Virginia, on Seminary Avenue. We lived on the corner at one end of the street, and my best friends Edwinette and Bonny Gray lived at the other end of the street. As children, probably around age seven or eight, one of our ways for determining love was by picking daisies. Like many other children of that day, we would pick and pull the petals off the flower and repeat these words, *He loves me, he loves me not, he loves me, he loves me not*, always hoping the final petal would prove love, but if not, we would run and grab a new daisy. Now that I'm older and have a better understanding of the love of God, when I see a daisy, I immediately think, *He loves me, He loves me more, He loves me, He loves me more, HE LOVES ME*. And nothing compares to His love.

I Love Me

Love yourself on purpose every day. Don't wait for someone to come and love you. You love you. Remind yourself you are enough. God made you. There is no other you in the world.

Be blessed, be happy, be loved, be you, and bless the good Lord who made you you.

Love Questions

1. How can you love on purpose today?
2. Who can you love on purpose today?
3. What is your love goal on purpose today?

Our Love Mission

Open the windows of your heart and let love shine big and bright every day.

Wake up and open your eyes of love on purpose.
Rise up and shine the light of love on purpose.
Get back up when you fall and love on purpose.
Stand up and fight for the right to love on purpose.
Level up love on purpose.

Crown up as royal children of love on purpose.
>Never give up on the journey of love on purpose.

March to the beat of love on purpose.
Never lose the wonder of love on purpose.
Raise the standard of love on purpose.
Always choose the way of love on purpose.
Rise to the occasion of love on purpose.
Step in the name of love on purpose.
Set the stage of love on purpose.
Stay on the path of love on purpose.
Spread the fragrance of love on purpose.
Taste the flavor of love on purpose.
Never stop the pursuit of love on purpose.
Never underestimate the power of love on purpose.
>Today and always, this is love, this is us.
>Love is free—throw that stuff around everywhere like confetti.
>Know what is love. Know what is *not* love.

Say I Love You on Purpose

First Corinthians 13:13 says, "Now abideth faith, hope and love, but the greatest of these is love."

"When asked the question, What is the greatest commandment, Jesus replied, 'Love the Lord your God with all your heart, with all your soul and with all your mind. The second is like unto it, love your neighbor as yourself (Matthew 26:36–39).'"

>When we say I love you, that's love on purpose.
>When we are kind, that's love on purpose.

When we give, that's love on purpose.
When we forgive, that's love on purpose.
When God forgave us, that was love on purpose.

When we help others, that's love on purpose.
When we visit the sick, that's love on purpose.
When we comfort the lonely, that's love on purpose.
When we take care of the children, that's love on purpose.
When we take care of our parents, that's love on purpose.
When we show up and shine, that's love on purpose.
Pray about everything, and keep your love light burning.
There is no love without God, and there's no God without love.
God is love. We are love.
We are free to
Love on purpose.
God help me to be
Love on purpose.
Amen.

Roz Brown

ROZ the ministry was birthed as she began preaching love to the lost in 1985. Her powerful and anointed presentation of the gospel through spoken word has afforded her the opportunity to bless the lives of many on national as well as international platforms as a sought-out preacher, teacher, psalmist, and speaker.

ROZ the elder is ordained in the International Christian Ministries, Richmond, Virginia, under her mother, presiding prelate and founder, her eminence, Chief Apostle Olive C. Brown. Roz serves in The I.C.M. as international psalmist, a pastor of worship and an active member of The New Jerusalem ICM, in Richmond under the pastoral leadership of her brother and pastor, Bishop Joel Vincent Brown.

ROZ the psalmist has led thousands into intimate throne-room worship with the Almighty, through her passionate style of worship and praise in churches, concerts, and conferences for more than twenty years. Roz has served as psalmist/worship leader for various churches in and throughout the state of Virginia and around the United States. She has also been blessed to work and train with a host of world-renowned gospel artists around the globe. She routinely hosts a Night of Worship in Richmond, a service where worshippers gather to experience the raw, unrestricted presence of God.

ROZ the Love Multiplied Outreach Ministry has worked with area young adults in local schools training and sharing in music and ministry. She also ministers at various state and local correctional facilities where she gives spiritual counseling, support, and guidance through ministry.

ROZ the daughter was born into a legacy of preachers, pastors, and spiritual leaders as the second of five children to the union of the late Bishop James F. Brown Jr. and International Christian Ministries Presiding Prelate/Founder, Her Eminence Chief Apostle Olive C. Brown.

ROZ the Mom celebrates the joy of being the mother of her two

God-given angels/daughters, Chanel-Kirsten, a foster mother/teacher/behavioral therapist in Forest, Virginia, and Jasmine-Rochelle, a retail product designer/developer and stylist in Charlotte, North Carolina.

ROZ the YiaYia/Grand Mom loves her two amazing boys Zachary, Noah and all the Love Multiplied foster children God sees fit to place in their home and lives. They are all truly gifts from God, and the moments are precious, priceless, and never taken lightly.

ROZ the sister/friend enjoys fellowship and friendship with her natural and spiritual sisters and brothers. Through this, Her Soul Sister Sundays Ministry has been birthed, offering women monthly support, encouragement, and empowerment.

ROZ, her assignment, is to reach the lost according to Luke 14:23, "Go into the country roads and lanes and compel people to come in so that my house will be full."

ROZ, her message, is love, according to John 15:12, "This is my commandment: Love one another the way I have Loved you."

ROZ, her heart, is to be a true worshipper, as her joy and purpose in life is fulfilled through preaching, teaching, singing, and above all living the message of love, which draws men and women into a sincere relationship with God the Father.

Your Exit Strategy

SHARVETTE MITCHELL

It was a brisk October morning at almost lunchtime, and I was walking across the Richmond, Virginia, West Creek campus of Capital One Bank heading to a 10/10 with my manager. She had recommended that we have this 10/10 check in–style meeting over lunch. This type of meeting allows the associate to talk and share for half of the meeting and the manager to share and talk the other half. As I walked from my building to the Capital Yum (that's how they name the cafeterias), the Lord said, "It's time."

My manager and I met up and jumped in line to order miso soup with chicken and pork dumplings/wontons swimming around. As we sat down and enjoyed small talk and our lunch, I said, "I have something I want to talk about." Her face became blank for a few seconds. Perhaps she thought I had some negative feedback for her, or perhaps there was a project that was off the rails that I was bringing to her attention. Quite the contrary.

"I am ready to leave Capital One" were the words that flew out of my mouth.

At that moment, I felt a wave of peace rush over me. The actual weight of peace sat on me so heavy, like a person sitting in your lap. This was internal confirmation that I was making the right move in the next phase of my purpose.

My manager immediately perked up and asked a few questions about my outside endeavors and immediately became an advocate for me to assist with a successful transition out of what was now a twenty-five-year corporate career. Yes, you read that correctly. I was about to walk away from a twenty-five-year corporate career with a great salary, bonuses, benefits, perks, work-from-home status (way before the pandemic) to leap into full-time entrepreneurship *without* a lottery win or a rich husband—well, no husband.

This lunch conversation happened in October 2017, and by February 2, 2018, I walked out of the doors of Capital One Bank and never looked back. At the time of the printing of this book, I have celebrated five successful years as a full-time entrepreneur.

But as they do in the movies, let me back up and talk about how I got to this point.

It was a beautiful sunny day in October 1992. I parked my car in the parking lot of what was then known as Signet Bank (now Capital One Bank) as I prepared for an interview. This would be my first *real* job. I had worked in fast food, telemarketing, and bridal retail, but working at a bank would be the real deal for this live-at-home Virginia Commonwealth University (VCU) college student. As I walked up the sidewalk off West Broad Street in Richmond, Virginia, I said to myself, *This is the sidewalk I am going to walk on every day*. As I entered the building and went to the security desk, I said to myself, *This is the security guard I am going to say hello to each day*. I was speaking it into existence. Perhaps some call it affirmations or the law of attraction. I call it faith.

God gave me favor with the interviewer, and I landed the four-to-midnight call center associate job and started my career November 2, 1992. Little did I know that the same faith I walked in with October

1992 was the same faith I would walk out with twenty-five years later on February 2, 2018.

Since this was the call center and operations side of the bank versus a bank branch, there were lots of opportunity to move around laterally or get promoted. I went from a four-to-midnight call center associate, to a seven p.m. to seven a.m. overnight shift call center associate, to a nine a.m. to six p.m. day shift call center associate. I then moved to sales, collections, dispute correspondence, and finally into training and development. I spent the bulk of my twenty-five-year career in training and development focused on consumer compliance such as anti-money laundering (AML) and Bank Secrecy laws, privacy laws, insider trading, Fair Credit Reporting Act, et cetera.

* * *

"Wait. We can't print this stuff without putting a website address on it."

Those were the words I said early 2006 while sitting at the kitchen table of my friend Edwinette Moses. For the past few hours, we had worked on marketing materials such as business cards, brochures, and magnets for her new and budding side business. As we pulled up vistaprint.com on the computer to see printing options for the materials we'd created, I had enough foresight to push pause and stop us because I realized that Edwinette needed to put a website on these marketing materials. We had just one problem: She did not have a website.

"I can go figure that out."

After I created Edwinette's pink-and-green website, I turned to helping my church with its web presence. People then started asking me to help them build websites. I did two or three more *free* websites, and then I stopped and thought, *Don't people pay for this?* At this point, I realized I had a valid business. I was providing a solution to a problem that people had *and* would pay for.

This was the beginning of my side hustle or part-time business and the start of Mitchell Productions, LLC. So, during the day, I worked as an associate of Capital One Bank, and during the evenings and weekends, I put on my superwoman cape and created great websites for various clients. I then stepped into social media consulting because my web design clients needed a "next step" after their website was up and running. I immediately advised of leveraging social media and other marketing activities to get the word out about their company. I also started *The Sharvette Mitchell Radio Show*, which is now a livestream broadcast and podcast. I also started hosting business conferences for women, and I even had a celebrity guest speaker, Kim Coles from *Living Single!*

This worked well for a long time. I was content with my day job, my work, my directors and managers, and fellow coworkers while being thankful for the extra income that I always had from my side business. I have seen former coworkers get pregnant and then send that same child off to college. I have seen former coworkers be single, get married, get divorced, and get married again. I know that working in corporate America was a part of my overall purpose. It actually gave me skillsets that prepared me for being a full-time small business owner.

So let me insert some grace right here. Everyone who starts a business does not need to leave their job. You can be happy and content with doing both. It is a very individual process, so don't let any outside pressures or social media put you into "rush" mode.

Around 2015, I began to think and imagine what it would feel like to put all of my time and energy into Mitchell Productions. Could I make it out there on my own? Was I going to look back and have regrets that I did not at least try to do it? Was I good enough? I started feeling like I was in a box. I tossed around leaving corporate America, and I gave myself a few "leave" deadlines that I missed! So, when I heard God say, "It's time" as I walked to the 10/10 lunch with my manager in October 2017, I threw all cards on the table and bet on myself and God.

I am asked frequently, "How did you know it was time to leave?" and

"What did you do to prepare to leave?" I am going to share, for the first time, my exit strategy.

If you have the luxury of preparing your exit from your job, there are things that you can do to help with a smoother transition while accelerating your business.

Let me also say this: I am not insensitive to the fact that people get pink slips every day, companies downsize or close their doors, or spouses relocate families for a new opportunity. In these cases, you don't have preparation time. You may be thrust into full-time entrepreneurship for one of these factors, and it can be scary. Welcome to the party. I trust that you will find and receive grace for this entrepreneurial journey.

The upcoming guidance is slanted toward those who have the ability to plan and prepare their exit into the next dimension of their purpose by way of full-time entrepreneurship. I humbly submit my twelve component exit strategy.

1. Leave on good terms.

What is the word on the street about you at your job? That plays a factor into your overall personal brand and the reputation you carry beyond the doors of your job. You may be surprised to find out how small the world is. Your last manager or long-time coworker could refer business to you or be the person who sends a large contract your way. It may be tempting to zone out and just coast along when you have your eyes set on jumping into your entrepreneurial journey, however, I highly recommend that you leave on good terms. When I told my then-manager that I was ready to go, she made a comment that if it did not work out, I could probably get a job back at the company. To date, things have worked out, but it feels good to know that I left on good terms. In addition, your job and the skills you gained are not thrown in the trash when you leave. Those skills are transferable to your small business. They are a part of your preparation. In fact, I would encourage you to update your résumé *before* you plan to leave to capture your skills and accomplishments. If you step into corporate contracting, grant competitions or government contracting, you may still be asked for a résumé.

Lastly, find out *and* follow the process and options that you have for exiting a company. Attend exit interviews, follow resignation letter guidelines, et cetera.

2. Establish and start your business *now*.

I hear people say that when they leave their job, they are going to start a business or they are leaving a job *to* start a business. That is a gross mistake. You need to legally establish your business, start building your brand, and have paying customers before you exit. Building a business takes time. We are in this for a marathon race and not a sprint.

In addition, there are tons of things to learn from marketing, pricing, procedures, and processes, handling finances to delivering great products and services. Use this time while you are employed to learn some of these lessons and to make money. Yes, we are in business to make money. Most people find that they don't live paycheck to paycheck if they have a small business on the side. Your side business also gives you an indicator of your revenue potential when you do leave. For some people, the writing was on the wall because their side business income matched or exceeded their job income. This showed them a clear sign, "Exit here."

For me, my business income had *not* replaced my corporate income at the time I left, however, I had steady growth and a good livable amount. By the end of the first year of full-time entrepreneurship, I had matched my corporate salary. I attribute that to working my side business for almost nine or ten years in conjunction with my corporate career. That may not be your story or your timeline, but trust me, you should absolutely start your business and have paying customers while working your job.

3. Enlist your silent investor.

You can ease your transition to full-time entrepreneurship if you look at your job as a silent investor. I heard founder of Unstoppable Black Woman Donna Izzard say that. When you are starting *and* running a business, there are various expenses such as website design, web hosting, email marketing services, business cards, brochures, advertising, accounting software, appointment scheduling systems, calendar and project management tools, raw materials, products, packaging, contractors, virtual assistants, equipment, coaching, self-study courses, business consulting, et cetera. You have the *luxury* of having a job that probably pays for at least your living expenses, so if you don't make money in your small business for a month, you will still eat, drive, and have somewhere to live, right? This "silent investor" affords you the ability to invest money into your business to cover business expenses or re-invest your profit back into the business. Those who are full-time entrepreneurs do not have this option (unless there is a supportive spouse or other income).

While you are working and preparing for full-time entrepreneurship, get your limited liability company business structure, business license, contracts (lawyer services), accounting system (accountant services), photoshoots, logo, printer, marketing courses, business coaching, business systems, products, and the list goes on depending on your business. Think about items that are one-time purchases or purchases that will hold you over for a while. This will help with your future cash flow needs because you won't need to spend money on these items.

Lastly, your "silent investor" may offer benefits that will help you in your small business. Does your job offer tuition reimbursement? I am a proud graduate of VCU with a bachelor of science in marketing. I received tuition reimbursement for my sophomore year through senior year. Guess what? I never worked in the marketing department in corporate America, but my degree backs me up as a marketing consultant and backs up my company, Mitchell Productions, which is a marketing consulting firm that focuses on marketing, branding, and visibility for small businesses.

4. Step up your savings.

This part of the exit strategy is pretty cut and dry. Most people will recommend that you have at least three to six months of living expenses saved. The more you have saved for your living expenses and entertainment (you won't stop going to movies and concerts) and eating out expenses (you won't stop eating out), the easier you will breathe. It will help you talk yourself off the ledge when sales are moving slow. You can say to yourself, *If I don't make one more dime, I can continue to sustain myself for XX amount of time.* In addition, your business has monthly expenses, so I encourage you to have money saved in your business account(s) also. That's why tip two and tip three of the exit strategy are important.

Do you get bonuses, tax return refunds, et cetera? Consider sliding those into a personal savings account. Instead of spending the business revenue on your next big purchase, consider keeping that income in your business checking or savings account. *Please speak with an accountant for personal and specific financial guidance.*

When I left corporate America, I had money saved in the business account and a good amount in my personal savings account. And to this day, I still have money saved for the business and personal accounts. You decide what feels good and comfortable to you, but having money saved will help you to not operate in fear and lack but to operate in abundance.

5. Reduce debt and improve credit.

By reducing or eliminating debt, you reduce the amount of money you need to actually live. This dollar figure is important because for most people leaving a job to jump into full-time entrepreneurship, they want to enjoy a similar lifestyle. If your personal income is reduced due to entrepreneurship, but your debt is reduced as well, you may still have a similar lifestyle. Don't get me wrong, a lot of new full-time small businesses experience nothing but growth and increase in revenue and profits when they jump in. Matter of fact, that was my experience. However, for some, there is a ramp-up time for them to replace or exceed their current take-home income.

Leverage this time on your job to work on reducing or eliminating debt. This will also help with improving your credit. This is all about positioning and preparing you for your purpose. If you want or need to get a credit card for something business related, you don't want your credit to be the hindrance. I know there is a lot of conversation on the streets about business credit. *Please speak to a financial specialist about that.* In my experience, when you are starting as a full-time entrepreneur, lenders are looking at *your* credit. Why? Because you are the one handling the money. Credit tells the lender about your past behavior.

I am proud to say that I left corporate America with good credit, and my credit score has increased.

6. Strategize your home front.

Purchasing a home has a lot of moving parts like finding the perfect home, down payments, credit, debt-to-income ratio, interest rates, inspections, appraisals, et cetera. The common consensus is that purchasing a new home as a full-time entrepreneur is more challenging than the process is for a W-2 employee who has standard pay stubs and proof of income. The reason is that mortgage lenders want a higher level of confidence in your income along with the consistency and repeatability of that income. Remember, when you are in business, you have to make money, and you have to keep making money. With this information in your back pocket, you can be strategic about your home front.

If you were already planning on purchasing a new home, or you have outgrown where you are, then it may be better to make the home purchase *before* you leave your job.

If you are renting, then you may decide this is still the best option for you. This is completely up to you. The main point is that you want to think about the home front and prepare to make a move or be okay with staying where you are for a few more years.

I had tossed around the idea of purchasing a new home before I left corporate America, but I decided to stay in my condo because it's manageable. My mortgage is fifty percent to sixty-five percent less than what most people pay in rent. I also had the equity in the condo as a backup plan if I needed it. To date, I have not needed it.

Oh, and let me mention home improvements. Don't forget to consider home improvements that you want or need to make. For example, will you work out of your home? Perhaps you need a workstation or a more robust home office. Be strategic about trying to take care of those improvements before you exit your job.

7. Ride in style.

Similar to the decision around your home is this discussion around your car. If you want or need a new (or new to you) car, it may be better to get the new car loan *before* you leave the job. I would have you challenge yourself around your real car needs. If your business will be operated out of your home, how much will you actually drive? On the flip side, if your business will require a ton more driving, product deliveries, or out-of-town travel, do you need a van or a secondhand car, or do you need the luxury car that is calling your name every time you ride by the dealer? This is a no judgment zone. The decision is yours. My main point is that you intentionally prepare for your exit and prepare for your next level.

When I left the job February 2, 2018, I only had four more car payments to make. By May 2018, I was free from that bill and debt. This brought down my living expenses, which we talked about earlier. As of the writing of this chapter, I have not purchased a new car, and I still ride in style.

8. Map out your 401(k) options.

If you have contributed to a 401(k) retirement plan at your job, you will need to do something with that money when you exit the job. Work with a financial planner to map out your retirement goals and what to actually do with the money. To my surprise, my financial planner was able to move the 401(k) money into three different directions. I was not aware of that. Start asking the questions now, and find someone licensed that you trust.

If you are considering taking the money in your 401(k) to fund your business, talk to a tax professional about tax implications.

9. Plan for health insurance.

Based on people I have talked to, health insurance is the main reason they do not step into full-time entrepreneurship. I get it. It is scary, and it is an additional bill you are adding to your living expenses. As a full-time entrepreneur, you will need to decide how you want to handle your medical needs and health insurance. There are a few things to consider.

Do you have a spouse who can cover the insurance? If you do, you are in a good place.

Are there any temporary medical benefits available to you from your employer once you leave? Per wikipedia.org, The Consolidated Omnibus Budget Reconciliation Act of 1985 (COBRA) is a law passed by the U.S. Congress on a reconciliation basis and signed by President Ronald Reagan, which, among other things, mandates an insurance program that gives *some* employees the ability to continue health insurance coverage after leaving employment.

Is your income and mindset at a place where you can pay out of pocket for medical expenses *when or if* they occur? I know of small business owners who take this approach and pay out of pocket for medical expenses.

For most people, having medical insurance is something they want, so guess what? We pay for it. There are options available through the Affordable Care Act. You can also talk to an insurance broker about options. Be sure to talk to an accountant about tax implications that may be in your favor related to the insurance premiums you pay.

I have and continue to maintain medical, dental, and vision insurance. Is it a bill that I did not have before leaving corporate America? Yes. Does my business make profit to afford me to pay it? Also yes.

10. Shift your mindset.

Mindset really does matter in this discussion about preparing for your purpose. Dictionary.com defines mindset as *the established set of attitudes held by someone.* What you will find as you start operating your business on the side while at your job is that you are now a double agent. One side of you is the employee, and the other side of you is the business owner and current/future employer. At some point, there will be a baton pass from the employed you to the self-employed you. This will first start in your mind and attitude.

Begin feeding your mind the nutrients it needs to believe, hope, embrace faith and possibility, dream, imagine, declare, and think. This may look like prayer, scriptures, affirmations, podcasts, therapy, journaling, music, et cetera. Why do you need this? Because what full-time entrepreneurs don't talk about enough are the fears, doubts, questions, anxieties, imposter syndrome, and rejection you will feel from time to time. *Did I make the right decision? Was this the right time? What if I don't sell anything else? What will happen six months from now? Should I just go find a job?*

I want to encourage you to bet on yourself and lean on GOD. Give yourself a chance. Get your mindset and faith in a place that anything is possible and that you are open to receive all of the good coming your way.

Here are examples of affirmations I created and use. I even had them printed on cards and gave them to some clients and my conference attendees:

- I have clarity and focus every day.
- I am effective and productive every day.
- I am a highly sought-after resource every day.
- I am my customer's solution every day.
- I have high-paying clients who enjoy working with me every day.
- I generate revenue every day.
- I am building a legacy every day.
- I am loved and cherished every day.

In addition to these affirmations, there are declarations and prayers specific to business that I lean on and that help me.

Do affirmations actually work? According to healthline.com, *Neuroplasticity, or your brain's ability to change and adapt to different circumstances throughout your life, offers a clue to help understand not only what makes affirmations work, but how to make them more effective.*

Your brain sometimes gets a little mixed up on the difference between reality and imagination, which can be surprisingly useful.

Regular repetition of affirming statements about yourself can encourage your brain to take these positive affirmations as fact. When you truly believe you can do something, your actions often follow.

11. Rev up your internal support system.

I define your internal support system as your immediate family—whether they live with you or not. As you prepare your exit to this next part of your purpose, your family will feel impacts. That may look like constraints on your time or that may mean they will see you more. That may look like less dining out or more spontaneous weekend trips to the mountains or beach. That may mean they will need to cook more of the holiday meals, or that may mean you want to do an out-of-the-box holiday. That may mean that they need to carry the financial weight for a while or that things are going great and you want them to come work in your business. I think you get the point. There will be impacts. My hope is that you have and feel support from your internal support system because they have seen you working your exit strategy. Involve them as much as you can. Let them in on the plan.

My mother was really the only person I was concerned about with my transition to full-time entrepreneurship. I did not want her to worry. When I first told her that I was going to leave a job I had worked at twenty-something years, she said, "What? Maybe you should wait." I get it. Her generation stayed on jobs until retirement. Matter a fact, my mom retired as a registered nurse with forty-five years of faithful service to St. Mary's Hospital in Richmond, Virginia.

By working my exit strategy, I was able to ease her fears. Trust me, she is my biggest supporter and cheerleader. Just stop by my social media pages. You will see her comments and show of support.

Let me say this: I do realize that some of you reading this book do not have support from your internal support system. It is something that I see and hear on social media. There are many factors that my chapter can't address. My guidance to you is this: Do not internalize their lack of faith, trust, or support as an indicator about your business or the direction of your goals.

Check out the final component of my exit strategy for an additional source of support.

12. Build your squad.

Outside of your family, there is a squad of support that can help you mentally prepare for your exit.

Faith Leaders

Early fall of 2017, my pastor, Bishop Joel V. Brown, preached a sermon about ravens. Specifically, he shared from 1 Kings 17:4–6 (NKJV): "'And it will be that you shall drink from the brook, and I have commanded the ravens to feed you there.' So he went and did according to the word of the LORD, for he went and stayed by the Brook Cherith, which flows into the Jordan. The ravens brought him bread and meat in the morning, and bread and meat in the evening; and he drank from the brook."

Well, this one phrase jumped up out at me: *I have commanded the ravens to feed you there.* It was like God was giving me specific confirmation that I would be okay. It was my assurance that I was going in the right direction with my exit strategy and that He would take care of me. My pastor did not know that sermon was for me, but it was. Even to this day, I lean on that scripture, and God has stood up to His promise of commanding my blessing.

After I told my mom about my plans to exit corporate America, I then told my spiritual leaders and pastors, Bishop Joel V. Brown and Chief Apostle Olive C. Brown. I received immediate support. If you are faith based, you will want and need the prayers and well wishes of your faith community.

Friends

I remember telling one friend about my plans, and I immediately heard and felt their fear. From that point on, I was very selective in the additional people that I told about my plans to transition to full-time entrepreneurship. I did not want anyone else's fear to jump on me.

However, I did have three or four friends that I told about the exit strategy and received immediate support and declarations of "You can do it." So, I am not saying that you need to shout it from the rooftop, but identify a few key friends that you can trust to morally support you in this journey.

Other Business Owners

Social media gets a bad rap for being a "messy" place for some. That has not been my experience. I have always been able to connect and find likeminded business owners, peers, and customers because of social media.

Other business owners can be an incredible source of support and camaraderie. They are all over Facebook, Facebook groups (like www.HeyGirlHey.today), TikTok, Twitter, Instagram, LinkedIn, and other online sources. Find your tribe and grow there with them. This may include networking in your local city, attending business brunches and conferences, or even joining a group coaching program like The Platform Builder program (PlatformBuilder.biz).

So there you have it. The twelve components of my exit strategy from corporate America into full-time entrepreneurship. *I have no regrets.* More importantly, I know without any doubt that this was all a part of God's plan for my life. My purpose was unfolding right in front of me and it still is. Every step I have taken has prepared me for the next step. I accepted my invitation to the next level and I hope you will also.

Sharvette Mitchell

Sharvette Mitchell works with small businesses to enable them to build their marketing strategy so that they generate more revenue with an amazing brand. She does this by focusing on their visibility, marketing, and branding through one-on-one consulting; group coaching programs based on her trademarked framework, The Platform Builder; speaking; and events.

Sharvette is a graduate of Virginia Commonwealth University with a bachelor of science in marketing. She brings to the table twenty-five years' past experience in corporate America in the field of training and development and consumer compliance for a global bank.

Sharvette has been featured in publications such as AARP, Huffington Post, HOPE for Women magazine, CEO Magazine, Rescue A CEO blog and SistaSense Magazine. Sharvette has also been seen on CBS 6 Monday Motivation, CBS 6 Virginia This Morning, The CW Network, and Comcast Cable.

In addition, she is an ICF Professional Certified leadership coach, a past member of the board of directors of James River Writers, and a former recipient of the ACHI Magazine's Radio Personality of the Year Award.

Since 2008, she has hosted a weekly talk radio show, The Sharvette Mitchell Radio Show, which airs on Blog Talk Radio, Apple Podcast, iHeart Radio, and on her five live streaming platforms. Lastly, Sharvette is the visionary author of five book collaborations, Propel, Pour, Pursue, Pearls and Prepare for Purpose. Learn more at www.Mitchell-Productions.com.

www.ingramcontent.com/pod-product-compliance
Lightning Source LLC
Chambersburg PA
CBHW071856070526
44583CB00016B/1722